3-1-55

The Secret

of

Effective Prayer

The Secret

of

Effective Prayer

by

HELEN SMITH SHOEMAKER

FLEMING H. REVELL COMPANY

To my Father and Mother

SENATOR H. ALEXANDER SMITH

and

HELEN DOMINICK SMITH

whose adventurous faith keeps them

forever young of heart

888437

Introduction

BOOKS ON PRAYER ARRANGE THEMSELVES IN VARIOUS CATEGORIES
and classes. Some are scholarly tomes which for the layman
are dry and impractical. Some are so mystical in character that
only certain types of minds and temperaments can possibly understand them. Some emphasize narrow theological ortho-
doxies. Some are so broad and visionary that they merely
promote wishful thinking, while others of a more modern
version are geared down to such a low level of ideology that
the Cross is left out completely and individual health and happiness seem to be the only goal.

Obviously there are many wonderful books on prayer, but
still it is hard to find one that is practical enough for the
average layman to utilize in his daily human experience. It
seems to me that Helen Shoemaker has done an excellent job
in this latter direction, for her book is geared to the needs of
people who want to know when to pray, how to pray, where
to pray, and what to pray. This is a usable book. For many
who are familiar with various fields pertaining to the subject,
it may seem too elementary. Yet I have rarely seen a scholar
who knew so much about prayer that he couldn't learn from a
simple manual for beginners. It seems to me that almost anyone can benefit from this approach.

I am always interested in the people who write books on prayer. What are they like? Are they people who really pray, or are they individuals who spend most of their time studying the subject rather than being deeply immersed in its practice and operation. Helen Shoemaker is anything but a theorist on the subject. She is a dynamic woman of vast energy who is constantly seeking to apply it more perfectly to her own needs and to the benefit of others.

I have watched the author organize prayer groups; her effectiveness is indeed marked. She has touched many people in the city of Pittsburgh and its environs and has brought them together in small circles for the purpose of prayer, study and fellowship. Among the people with whom she works are to be found some of those you would least expect to be interested in such a program. She has touched every kind of personality, from the rich and sophisticated to the poor and unlettered. Thus, she writes out of an experience that I know is factual and workable.

I am confident that the richness of her background as a spiritual activist will be able to communicate much to those who read her book. The book deals with Christian beginnings and personal contacts with God and one another. It does not attempt to go into the social implications of the Gospel, although they are definitely intimated. She certainly is not a woman who believes that "right thinking" and faith will solve everything. She is fully aware of the fact that prayer is only a starting point and that it must result in action—the kind of action that feeds the hungry, administers justice to the abused, and seeks to encourage righteousness wherever it is absent.

Austin Pardue,
Protestant Episcopal Bishop of Pittsburgh

Pittsburgh, Pennsylvania

Contents

9

PART III

PART I

The only way to avoid calamity is to take the offensive.

ELTON TRUEBLOOD

CHAPTER I

The World We Live In

As WE GLANCE AT OUR WORLD, WE SEE WHOLE CONTINENTS IN
ferment. Everywhere there is restlessness, conflict, danger.
There are several reasons for this.

One is the smoldering upthrust of underprivileged peoples,
especially in Africa and Asia, seeking freedom and independ-
ence.

The second reason for this world ferment is that wherever
this upthrust begins to show itself, the sinister hand of the
Kremlin reaches out and stirs unrest to its own advantage.

Reinhold Niebuhr, noted Protestant theologian, spoke
prophetically when he warned the assembly of the World
Council of Churches at Amsterdam:

When anyone speaks comparatively and presents the Soviet
system as a possible alternative to democracy, we must insist that

he has not dealt with the real tragedy of our age. That consists in the horrible evils generated by the Communist alternative to our civilization. Hell knows no fury like that of a prophet of a secular religion become the priest-king of a Utopian state. Our civilization may be faulty, but the alternative is much worse. The ramparts of our civilization may be tattered, but they contain defenses of freedom which require that we support them against this new fury.

Sir Winston Churchill, at the mid-century convocation of the Massachusetts Institute of Technology on April 1, 1949, defined the real nature of Communism with alarming accuracy and foresight:

> We may well ask, "Why have they [the Russians] deliberately acted so as to unite the free world against them?" It is because they fear the friendship of the West more than its hostility.
>
> Thirteen men in the Kremlin, holding down hundreds of millions of people and aiming at ruling the world, feel that at all costs they must keep up the barriers. Self-preservation, not for Russia, but for themselves, lies at the root, and is the explanation of their sinister and malignant policy.
>
> These thirteen men in the Kremlin have their hierarchy and a church of communist adepts whose missionaries are in every country as a fifth column, awaiting the day when they hope to be absolute masters of their fellow countrymen. . . . They have their anti-God religion. . . . Behind this stands the largest army in the world, in the hands of a government pursuing imperialist expansion as no Czar or Kaiser had ever done.

Since this time, leaders of Church and State have bombarded us with similar warnings. A procession of Secretaries of State in our own nation, and the UN leaders of the free nations, have shown endless patience and long-suffering in their efforts to turn the men of the Kremlin from their evil designs. But no human effort, no human wisdom, has been able to stop this spreading evil. The only good any of it has done is to clear the air of the fog of confused thinking in which we have been living since World War II. The rank and file of the people of the United States are reluctantly being forced to see that:

To the men of the Kremlin, might makes right, men are meant to be governed by other men. There is no God.

Twenty-five years ago Nicolai Lenin outlined the Communist objective:

When the 800,000,000 of Asia unite with us, the real revolution will blaze forth.

The terrifying accuracy of this strategy is highlighted by the recent events in China and Korea.

For the first time in history the entire population of the earth can be imperiled by ruthless men at any point on its surface. We have come into the stormy latitudes of history—the strong chance is that many now living must accommodate themselves to the prospect of living all their days in the midst of strain.[1]

A third reason for world unrest and mounting fear is the accelerating atomic armaments race, and the terrifying possibility that if World War III should break out, it could mean the actual destruction of civilization as we know it. Again to quote Dr. Trueblood:

Millions are fatalistic. They feel utterly powerless in the presence of forces which they can neither understand nor control. In spite of our proud achievements . . . there is a widespread sense that we are waiting for catastrophe.[2]

We sympathize with the cry of despair wrung from the lips of an unknown atomic age poet when he expressed "the widespread sense that we are waiting for catastrophe" in the following gloomy lines:

These are the last songs we shall ever sing together,
This is the last kindness we shall do;
Last roses, fragrant wood smoke in November
Last sea-blue sky of winter, summer lavender, green April weather,
Lilacs at night
              . . . no one will whisper to us
There will be no one to whisper to—
Only silence; not even forgetting.
Farewell, Farewell. It is unlikely that anyone hereafter
Will ever again speak Russian or English or Japanese,
Or have our kind of thoughts, our kind of anguish
Or dress for dinner, or go to afternoon teas.
All at an end now, the dream, the rust, the corrosion.
The long fever and chill,
Though there is still time left to capture, to try to recall
Something that was important—what was it? Taxes?
Or Nelson at Trafalgar? Or Rome in her might?
Or the way we cleared our fields with Connecticut Axes?
Or what somebody said in Galilee on a hill?
Whatever it was, I think you had better hurry,
Before it ends Completely, once and for all.
And there is no one left to talk to, and worry,
Not even to ask, Did you hear the last explosion?
Did you see the light?

                                       —Anon.

Human nature, especially the sorely tried human nature of such a harried world, shrinks from facing these stark facts and possibilities. The devils of doubt and compromise attack us. Is freedom worth having if we must risk another war to save it? Will it, in fact, survive another war? There must be some expedient that our statesmen have not yet tried to stave off the threatened cataclysm!

We forget that it is too much trust in desperate expedients and too little faith in the power of moral principle and spiritual force that caused our statesmen at Yalta, Tehran, and Potsdam to trade right for time, and thus hurried us to the brink of the abyss. The terrible indictment uttered by Winston Churchill after the Munich Conference preceding World War II rings in our uneasy ears: "Gentlemen, you have chosen between war and dishonor. You have chosen dishonor, you shall have war!"[7]

Are those words perhaps prophetic? While the wind is rising and the storm clouds pile up, the eternal cosmic warfare between good and evil in this our day seems to be focusing for a final collision beyond the power of any man or even group of men to stop.

This menacing world scene, then, presents a serious challenge to the courage and faith of all Christians. If we were stronger in our faith, clearer in our minds, and stauncher in our courage, we would meet this challenge head on.

Unfortunately the Christian people are not at present singing songs of triumph. We are slowly gathering our forces and recapturing the lost power and radiance of our faith, but the frightening headlines in the newspapers tend to influence us more than the glorious promises of Jesus and the prophets.

It is, therefore, urgent that we be reminded once again that God's power is greater than the power of the Kremlin; it is greater than the power of millions of marching men; it is greater than the atom and hydrogen bombs. We modern Christians need to turn back the pages of history and rediscover that the Christians have always outthought and outprayed and outlived the pagan world. The world needs a transfusion of faith in God and the courage to fight with His weapons.

CHAPTER 2

Dynamic Faith Is The Answer

IT WAS NAPOLEON BONAPARTE, THE TERROR OF EUROPE, WHO SAID: "There are only two forces in the world—spiritual force and material force, and spiritual force always wins." Napoleon died a prisoner on the island of St. Helena. His dreams of world conquest died with him, mute testimony to the fact that he had used the wrong weapons.

Twenty-five hundred years before Napoleon, a prophet of Israel, facing with unflinching courage the conquest of his nation by the great King of Babylon, looked with eyes of faith beyond that peril to a future triumph, and cried out his encouragement to his people:

Arise, shine; for thy light is come, and the glory of the Lord is risen upon thee. For, behold, the darkness shall cover the earth, and gross darkness the people; but the Lord shall arise

18

upon thee, and his glory shall be seen upon thee. And the Gentiles shall come to thy light, and kings to the brightness of thy rising (Isaiah 60:1,3).

Babylon is gone, Rome is only a memory, the kings and conquerors with their armies and banners have marched across the world stage and passed on into history, their kingdoms and empires have risen and waned and fallen. No one remembers what they said or even what most of them did, but the words of Isaiah are immortal. Only the glory of God has remained, and its radiance has spread with the centuries.

The people of God, filled with His power, literally did outlive, outthink and outpray the pagan world. They overcame the Roman Empire's effort to destroy them, and finally won the pagan world to their faith. They were the one light of the dark ages. They kept learning, art, and morals alive when the barbaric hordes from the North and East threatened to destroy all the inherited culture of the past. In some of humanity's most turbulent days, St. Augustine, St. Jerome, St. Francis, St. Thomas Aquinas, Erasmus, Luther, and millions of other dimly remembered saints, wise men, and prophets, carried the golden thread of pure faith through the centuries down to our time. These men and women have spread the light into every corner of the world. This is the great miracle of history.

Wars cannot destroy the power of this faith, dictators cannot suppress it. It is beaten out in one spot only to burst out into brighter flame in another.

It might be well for evil men to study history before they try to stamp out religion and launch their campaigns of world conquest. When men make war on the living God they do so not only to the peril of their immortal souls, but of their lives. The prophetic words of Jesus, spoken to St. Peter on the hills of Galilee, are still true: "Upon this rock [of your faith in me]

I will build my church and the gates of hell shall not prevail against it" (Matthew 16:18).

History testifies that spiritual force always wins in the end, because spiritual force issues from the Lord of Life Himself.

CHAPTER 3

Some Obstacles to Faith and How to Overcome Them

SPIRITUAL FORCE HAS NEVER WON AUTOMATICALLY, HOWEVER. Those who care to take a backward look into the past will notice that there never has been a time when great world forces were not contending for the mastery.

The people of faith always have had to establish the Christian way against terrific odds. They have been a minority withstanding and conquering pagan faiths, superstition, temporal rulers, and persecution.

Christ never promised His people the type of security that would release them from suffering, sacrifice, or struggle. No, He put into our hands His weapons of prayer, love, and power, and promised us that if we used them as He commanded nothing could withstand us.

Spiritual force, then, will continue to win and conquer the enemies of our happiness and freedom when enough people come to believe in it. There are many obstacles in our minds to overcome before we can exercise this spiritual force.

When I suggested to some friends of mine recently that powerful continuous and concentrated prayer could save us, one of them turned to me and remarked, "Then why hasn't prayer been able to head off the last two world wars? Perhaps evil is stronger than God."

Let us face it. Why hasn't prayer been able to head off the recent two world wars? No dogmatic answer to this question can be made, but it might possibly be somewhat as follows: Perhaps there are more of the world's people filled with fear and hatred, pride and doubt, than there are people who trust God and pray. I have already high-lighted the fact that the very air of the world we breathe is heavy with fear and foreboding.

"Events justify it," you might reply.

To which one might answer: "Your accumulated fears and hatreds might possibly be helping to precipitate those events."

Thought transference has been proven as a scientific fact. Your thoughts and my thoughts can influence the thoughts of others more than we realize. Parents have proved over and over how strongly their thoughts of fear or faith can influence their children, often subconsciously.

Is it not simple logic, then, to deduce that if the majority of the world's people are confused and fearful the state of mind of the world will be profoundly affected by it? Unless we Christians are strong enough in our faith to launch spiritual force against this great weight of dark thoughts, we will be conquered by them.

Devil-filled men know how to make capital for their own ends of the doubts and fears and hatreds of the masses, the result of which is always turmoil and war. When a person is tired and fearful that person is susceptible to disease. When society is tired and fearful it also is susceptible to disease. Revolution and war are diseases as destructive to the body politic as cancer is to our physical bodies.

Jesus showed us the way to avoid wars, but we have refused to learn from Him. He gave us two great commandments—to love God with all our hearts and souls and minds and strength, and our neighbors as ourselves.

Jesus' whole life illustrated these two commandments. He loved and obeyed God with His whole heart and mind and soul, and He loved and served people with no thought of self. He never responded negatively or resentfully or doubtingly to any situation with which life faced Him. He was all positive. In short, He was a perfect channel through whom God could act, and He asks us to be channels through whom God can act. War and revolution are the result of nations and individuals which did not wish to learn the great spiritual laws Jesus taught.

The second question, "Is evil stronger than God?" follows naturally on the first.

If evil were stronger than God, He would never have sent His Son to show us how to overcome it. God in His wisdom knew that evil could be defeated. God, in the person of His Son, faced the cruel facts of evil and pain and death unflinchingly for us. The crucifixion was the seeming triumph of evil, and God allowed it. The resurrection, however, was God's secret weapon and with it He triumphed by demonstrating His power to replace evil, suffering, and death with the creative force of love and life. The resurrection tells more about God and His power to overcome evil than any other event in history.

But still you are not satisfied. If God has infinite power and infinite love, why does He allow the terrible things that daily menace our loved ones and our own happiness and security? Why are there hurricanes, earthquakes, fires, famine, disease, accidents? No human being or combination of human beings can begin to explain or solve the whole mystery of human suffering. The greatest minds in history have struggled with the problem of pain.

God's explanation is Jesus. He is like the shaft of light which a lighthouse throws on a black, turbulent sea. As we come into the beam of this light, through faith and prayer, we begin to understand.

God sent Jesus, not to take all the insecurity and danger and challenge from life, but to teach us to live and pray so that we might joyfully cry with St. Paul: "This is the victory that overcometh the world, even our faith" (I John 5:4).

CHAPTER 4

Faith Is Stronger than Fear

THERE IS A PASSAGE FROM ST. PAUL'S LETTERS THAT SEEMS TO have been written especially for us. As we face our modern hour of peril, St. Paul and his handful of new Christians were facing extinction by imprisonment, torture, and death. Struggling as they were to hold a beachhead in the antagonistic pagan world of their day, they must often have quailed and been tempted to renounce their faith as too costly in the face of these terrifying possibilities. No doubt St. Paul got many letters from his Roman converts expressing their doubts and fears. His reply is magnificently summed up in the closing verses of the eighth chapter of Romans: Nay, in all these things we are more than conquerors through him that loved us. For I am persuaded that neither death, nor life, nor angels, nor principalities, nor powers, nor things present, nor things to come,

25

nor height nor depth, nor any other creature shall be able to separate us from the love of God which is in Christ Jesus our Lord (Romans 8:37-39).

St. Paul doesn't tell his frightened people to escape from all their troubles by denying that they exist. He doesn't tell them to avoid them by compromising with Rome. He doesn't tell them that Jesus will magically protect them from sorrow and suffering and danger. No! He tells them to look steadfastly at every awful possibility and to know that whatever they may be asked to go through, God will be with them to give them courage and peace and, more than that, conquering power. If nothing can conquer our spirits, then nothing can conquer us. There is nothing to fear but fear.

Only fear and unrepentance and disunity can destroy America now. England went to her knees in earnest and humble faith before the great retreat from Dunkirk in World War II, and God stretched forth His mighty arm and saved her.

Recently I was talking with a friend on the telephone. "I don't know what is to become of us," she said. "My son is in the active reserves, and my daughter-in-law is behaving very badly. If he is called up, I don't know what she will do. Her emotion has run away with her reason; she is obsessed with fear and resentment. What can we do to restore perspective to such people? It seems to me that our greatest national need at present is to get free of ourselves and our fears."

My friend is right. Let us look at the things that defeat us in the light of St. Paul's ringing promise. It is characteristic of St. Paul to name the final enemy first—death. We will all die some day, either by disease, accident, old age, or war. Death is a fact. There is no escaping it. Therefore, the way we die is more important than when we die. If only we could come to believe that "death is a physical incident through which life passes" it would be much less terrifying.

A man I knew died recently of cancer. He had no family, and few friends. As he lay dying in the ward of a city hospital, he told my husband that he would welcome death, not as deliverance, but as the beginning of the great adventure of Life. He had not been a good man, but in his illness he had found faith and freedom from fear. The Bible became for him the Book of books because it introduced him to a God who cared, a God whom he could trust, a God who would carry him through his ordeal, as He had carried Jesus through His, into the dawn of His Easter morning.

This man came to believe St. Paul: "That the sufferings of this present time are not worthy to be compared with the glory which shall be revealed in us" (Romans 8:18). He lost all fear of the painful process of death by cancer. His only fear was that under the pressure of pain his courage might waver, and he would dishonor his God by crying out. His death was an inspiring going, because above all the physical agony of his dying body his spirit soared glad and free. Even dying in pain could not separate him from the love of God, or the tingling expectancy of ongoing life.

A young soldier who was wounded in Korea wrote to his parents the following challenging account of his personal conquest of fear:

The attitude that the majority of soldiers, myself included, have adopted is a sensible one—pragmatic and workable. It is this. Do not worry about the future; it is beyond your control. Concern yourself only with those details necessary for your day-to-day existence, and work to bring about conditions advantageous to you, as that part of the future which you can see is unraveled. Improve your position; see how much you can organize better and look for ways to make the daily tasks easier. In your spare time do not dwell on morbid speculation; allow your mind to think only of the light and pleasant things. The benefits of this state of mind are twofold, and the disadvantages none. First, you do not live in a state of mental hell, and, second, because your mind and nerves are steady as a result of this attitude you are better equipped for a crisis, and hence you are better able to survive.

There are two types of hell: mental and physical. Life in Korea is quite comfortable physically except when on patrols. Mental hell is hell because it envisages physical suffering for the most part. To envisage physical suffering is a game for fools; to suffer physically is hell enough, dual suffering is unnecessary. Besides, your worst fears are never realized.

This is a roundabout way of saying what the soldier said when questioned if he was scared during an artillery bombardment. 'If one of those damned things (referring to a jagged piece of steel four or five inches long) gets me, well, it gets me, but if it doesn't, it doesn't, and I'm sure my worrying about it won't faze it in the least.'

You see, I used to worry terribly; prior to my being assigned to my company I spent several nights back in regimental rear with those brave, brave soldiers. Their war stories scared me stiff, but I found that while on line, since I had ceased to worry, I was never scared. Even while enacting my own war story I wasn't scared except for twenty seconds or so after I was hit—even then it was more surprise (unwarranted I'll admit) than fear. This attitude of mine and others works. It stood the test! Fear and worry are mental and hence can be controlled and in most cases eliminated.

Analyze what I've said and you must surely agree. Analyze death itself and it's not so horrible. The worst that can happen is that I die, and die I surely shall, as all of us must, but I won't die in Korea; at least statistics indicate the chances are against it. Why fear the inevitable? Sooner or later it happens. Myself, I can't be bothered with thoughts of this type, and if you have any sense you can't be bothered with them either. If I don't worry and fret, you shouldn't. In fact, you don't have the right to! All I can say, and I said it when I walked back from the engagement, is: "Thank you, God, for letting me live." There is nothing more to say and nothing more to think about. Why allow yourself to be morbid and fearful. It is asinine to terrorize yourself.

Think over what I've said; it's something I never learned at home; I had to come to Korea to learn it.

In another letter to friends he wrote: "Something you said some months ago has stuck with me: 'It's not what happens to you and not what you have to face that really matters, but rather how you face it and how you measure up.' This is really the important thing. If a man can believe this and act accordingly, he's pretty well won the battle."

I was lunching recently with a young mother and she voiced the fear that lies in many people's hearts: "I don't fear death for myself, my husband or my child; but sometimes when I awaken in the night and think of the kind of dying it would be, should an atomic or hydrogen bomb be dropped on our city, my heart turns to water."

Many of us have husbands, sons, grandsons, who are being called into the service of our country. We would not be human if we did not rebel violently against all the awful possibilities that may lie in the future. We have denied ourselves many comforts and pleasures for their sakes. They and their happiness have been our reasons for living, and now the threat to them and to all our dreams and plans lies heavy on our hearts.

Plague and pestilence, battle, murder and sudden death are thrown into startling relief by the imminence of our present danger from bacteriological warfare and hydrogen bombs, and when we kneel to pray we say, "Good Lord, deliver us," with new fervor. So St. Paul's vision of victory in the 8th Chapter of Romans answers the cry of our frightened hearts. Inspired words always do, if we, through prayer, can make them our own.

CHAPTER 5

Taking the Prayer Offensive

NOT LONG AGO A WOMAN VOICED TO ME WHAT SEEMS TO BE THE universal longing in the hearts of all of us.

"If only I knew how to pray," she said. "If only I could believe that prayer works as you Christians say it does."

The whole British nation knew after Dunkirk that prayer not only worked, but worked miracles. A mother whose son is saved from threatened blindness knows that prayer works. Anyone who has experienced God's great gift of healing knows that prayer works. In answer to prayer the Holy Spirit goes into action to empower and guide doctors, nurses, parents, statesmen, military leaders—all of us.

Our most effective secret weapon against Russia right now is universal and continuous prayer. A spiritual renaissance among the God-fearing peoples of the world is more to be feared by Russia than hydrogen bombs. Over and over the power of God-filled men has been demonstrated to be overwhelming. The power of a faith-charged atmosphere is fear-inspiring to the forces of evil and darkness. As someone has said:

Prayer is a force as vital as electricity, a force that can be utilized only by those who love and trust God, and let the stream of their life purpose run along in the streams of His great will. When we put the drop of our tiny will into the stream of His deathless purpose, we may ask anything and it shall be done for us. When we abide in Christ, our tiny will becomes an atom in His almighty will, and in His name we speak spiritual continents into being.

Jesus tells us: "Whatsoever ye shall ask in my name that will I do, that the Father may be glorified in the Son. If ye shall ask anything in my name, I will do it" (John 14:13;14). He also says: "If ye abide in me, and my words abide in you, ye shall ask what ye will, and it shall be done unto you" (John 15:7). And: "For verily I say unto you, If ye have faith as a grain of mustard seed, ye shall say unto this mountain, Remove hence to yonder place; and it shall remove; and nothing shall be impossible unto you" (Matthew 17:20).

The man who quieted the storm, who walked on the water, who healed every kind of sickness, who brought the dead to life, who Himself stepped alive out of a tomb, told us to have faith to ask in His name. He has opened the way for us straight to the throne of God. Our password is prayer in His name.

Dr. E. Stanley Jones tells us: "In prayer you align yourself to the purpose and power of God and He is able to do things through you that He couldn't do otherwise. . . . For this is an open universe, where some things are left open, contingent upon our doing them. If we do not do them, they will never be done. So God has left certain things open to prayer— things which will never be done except as we pray."[3]

Prayer, then, is "Religion in action."[4] It is love in action. It is faith in action. And it works.

It was an autumn evening. A group of young couples were drinking coffee in an attractive New York apartment. The sparkling skyline of midtown New York stabbing the warm dark night provided a perfect backdrop for the scene. On the sofa next to me sat a personable young man, a college graduate, a veteran of World War II. The purpose of the gathering was to discuss our Christian responsibility in today's world.

"I'm not a Christian," the young man said to me wistfully. "I wish I were. You people have something I haven't got, but to my way of thinking it just doesn't stand up against the facts of life."

Only a week later this young man's wife telephoned my husband to say that he had just been taken to the hospital with polio. She asked for our prayers. We held a weekly service for healing in our church, and Tom was prayed for at that service. The wife, a person of very strong Christian faith, also called some of her friends and asked them to pray for Tom daily.

He was literally submerged in prayer.

Of course he was alone in an isolation hospital. He realized fully what it would mean if he were to be crippled for life. He was just getting established in business after his long war service; he had a wife and two children to support. Why had this terrible thing happened to him? Why?

In his loneliness and fear he suddenly began to crave to read the Bible. His wife sent him one, and he read over and over the story of Jesus. He read of Jesus' healing the blind man, the lame man, the nobleman's son, and the beautiful words of encouragement seemed to be calling to him across the centuries: "Come unto me, all ye that labour and are heavy laden, and I will give you rest" (Matthew 11:28). "I am the way, the truth and the life" (John 14:6). "I am come that they might have life, and that they might have it more abundantly" (John 10:10).

As he read, both the fever and the fear began to go. His doubts began to dissolve too. He wondered why he, in his puny pride, had ever dared to say, "It doesn't stand up to the facts of life." He realized that here in a hospital room, suffering from a dreadful disease, he had been ushered into the presence of a Person so wonderful and a Power so mysterious that there was nothing left for him to do but to say humbly: "Lord, I believe, help thou mine unbelief."

A month later a pale, thin young man walked through my husband's study door. "I don't know why I came," he said. "I guess it's because I'm looking for someone to thank."

Together he and my husband knelt, and the young man poured out his gratitude to the great God who had come to him in answer to the prayers of his wife and friends.

With his wife's joyful consent, this man has gone into the Christian ministry, another witness to the power of prayer and the greatness of God.

Tom is not an isolated example. All over the world other Toms and Louises are being touched to new life and power by the hand of the great Creator because someone is praying for them.

In a gripping book entitled *God's Underground*,[5] a Roman Catholic priest tells how he traveled in disguise into Russia, where he was told that there were millions of Christians secretly meeting for prayer and Christian fellowship. His most thrilling story is of being billeted in an NKVD barracks, disguised as an Army doctor. He carried the elements of the mass with him in an aspirin bottle and an iodine bottle, and celebrated mass every evening on his bed.

One evening he had just time to throw some papers over the elements as a young woman NKVD officer walked in. They sat down to talk. This young woman, who had been brought up in the anti-God schools of Russia, and had been fed from childhood on anti-God propaganda, opened the conversation by bringing up the question of religion. They talked most of the night.

The next day she brought her husband and some friends. At the end of the week eight members of the dreaded secret police were baptized into the Christian faith, and knelt with the priest for prayer, on the bare floor of the NKVD barracks. Perhaps the prayer you said as you mopped the kitchen floor or darned the socks or made the beds found its destination in the hearts of these NKVD officers and guided the Roman Catholic priest. Who knows?

Millions of people pray daily for the redemption of Russia. Our prayers must strengthen and encourage millions to continue their struggle for faith and freedom, and bring uncounted others, as God through His servant brought the NKVD officers, out of darkness into His marvelous light. What is happening in Russia is shrouded in mystery, but we know that God is acting, and acting with power.

Millions of people, too, are praying for a great spiritual awakening throughout the world. Behind the scenes in every nation are groups of unknown men and women praying. In the great struggle for men's minds and bodies which is taking place the people of prayer may well hold the real balance of power.

PART II

Earth and Heaven have yielded their secrets to those who cared enough not to rest until they had found the key.

ELTON TRUEBLOOD

CHAPTER 6

How to Approach God

"PRAYER IS THE SWORD OF THE SPIRIT," BUT HOW ARE WE, AVERAGE people like us, to learn to grasp this weapon and use it? We feel so inept when we try to pray, so ineffective, so inarticulate. Perhaps the reiteration of a few spiritual laws will help us.

If you really want to learn to pray with power, certain spiritual exercises are essential. Any potential singer knows how much time must be spent on breathing exercises and scales. Any potential golfer knows that there is no hope of ever playing good golf unless he or she is willing to spend hours practicing the drive, the approach, and the putt. Baseball players, mountain climbers, cooks, doctors, lawyers—all know there are certain rules, techniques, governing their profession or vocation. Unless they learn these techniques they will never become good singers or baseball players or doctors.

The first essential of effective prayer is time and regularity. It is not enough to pray merely when the spirit moves us, although the spirit will move us more and more frequently as we cultivate our relationship with God.

It is not enough to treat God like a fire brigade and wait for the fire to break out before calling Him to the rescue.

If we gave as little time and regularity to eating as we do to prayer, we should probably die of malnutrition. We spend two or three hours daily at our meals, and feel very virtuous if we spend twenty or thirty minutes daily at our prayers.

A Christian should be a person to whom Jesus is a living presence. He cannot become a living presence unless we cultivate our friendship with Him—seek Him out, study the things He says about Himself and life and us. In short, spend time with Him every day. Then prayer will become a reality to us, and open doors for us which, without prayer, will never open.

A friend of mine makes a comparison with human friendship. If we value a friend, we take the trouble to keep in touch with him. We write to him, telephone him; we do things for him that we know will please him. We invite him to our home and take care not to allow any misunderstandings to come between us.

Should we be less considerate of God? He stands ready to give us much more than the love and understanding and comfort of friendship—He stands ready to give us eternal joy and absolute victory. He will not force His attentions upon us, He will not force His way into our homes and hearts. Holman Hunt's great painting illustrates His attitude perfectly: "Behold, I stand at the door, and knock; if any man hear my voice, and open the door, I will come in to him and will sup with him, and he with me" (Revelation 3:20). He is there, standing at the door of our hearts, graciously waiting for us to invite Him in.

Shall each of us, then, make a compact with ourselves, to cultivate our relationship with Him? Take the trouble to rise a half hour earlier than formerly, pick up our Bible or some other book about Him, read about Him, think of Him, pray to Him? This puts us in the mood to open the door of our day and invite Him to share it with us.

It is not enough to ask Him to share our day with us, rather we should put our day and ourselves at His disposal, so that He may use us for His purposes. The very thought that He might wish to channel His greatness through our littleness fills us with awe and gratitude.

It is no accident that Jesus opened the Lord's Prayer as He did. This helps us to visualize God—in other words, know something of Him to whom we are addressing ourselves. That is why those who think of God as a vague first cause or merely as Creative Mind or the Source of all Energy do not ever understand how to approach God in prayer, as did the prophets and Jesus.

Jesus introduces us to God in one short inclusive sentence. "Our Father Who art in Heaven." If, as the mystics agree, worship brings revelation, then the first great expression of recognition in the Lord's Prayer is the height of revelation. Here Jesus presents us to God in all His personality, His majesty and His glory.

The phrase "Our Father" is perhaps the most hope-inspiring phrase in any language. "Our" is a great inclusive word. God is the father of us all. The whole human family is His creation—black, white, brown, yellow. He has given life to all His children, and endows us equally with the capacity to acknowledge Him. He cherishes the life He gives. Jesus describes this tenderly when He says: "But the very hairs of your head are all numbered" (Matthew 10:30).

God's Fatherhood, if we are to believe Jesus, is a great

eternal fact. However, we do not realize this until we acknowledge it. We all have human fathers, but we do not fully appreciate all that that word implies (if they are good fathers)
until we consciously acknowledge them, appreciate them,
honor and cherish them; then we enter into a relationship of
mutual trust and fellowship, which is priceless.

I am one of those fortunates with a wonderful father. As
a child, I took his humor and tenderness, his understanding and
wisdom for granted. When I became older, however, I began
to realize that real friendship is not a one-way street, it requires
response. When I gave back to him, to the best of my ability,
the understanding and appreciation which he had always
given me, our relationship flowered into a rich unity of spirit.

Jesus used the familiar word, "father," because that word
is a fact in all our lives. We understand what it should mean
even if, in our human frailty, we have failed to give it meaning.

But Jesus sweeps our minds up and beyond to a further
revelation of what He means by Father. He says: "I and my
Father are one" (John 10:30). "He that hath seen me hath
seen the Father" (John 14:9). In other words, "I am God's
mirror to you. I am He in human form. If you cannot visualize
Him, look at me, my claims, my teaching, my quality of life.
In me you will see him."

Then Jesus adds the phrase, "who art in heaven." There
is nothing written that so graphically describes the majesty of
"Our Father in heaven" as the first few verses of the sixth
chapter of Isaiah. As you will remember, Isaiah, the prophet,
as a young man, was in the temple at prayer, when he saw a
vision which he describes with glorious imagery.

In the year that King Uzziah died I saw the Lord sitting
upon a throne, high and lifted up, and his train filled the temple.
Above him stood the seraphim; each had six wings: with two

he covered his face, and with two he covered his feet, and with two he flew. And one called to another and said: "Holy, holy, holy is the Lord of hosts; the whole earth is full of his glory." And the foundations of the thresholds shook at the voice of him who called, and the house was filled with smoke (Isaiah 6:1-4. RSV).

What a picture of the majesty and glory of God. Jesus wishes us to see this same picture, so in the phrase, "Who art in heaven," he lifts our sights heavenward, after focusing them on so familiar a word as Father.

Here is God in His universal aspect—the creator and director of the universe and of life; the fountainhead of divine energy. Mind above all minds. Wisdom above all wisdom. Power above all power. Light above all light. Love beyond all love. No wonder we fall to our knees in worship and adoration.

William Temple, the late Archbishop of Canterbury, said that "the name is the manifested nature."[6] Therefore, when we say, "Hallowed be thy name," we are revering and praising His nature as it has been revealed to us. No one has ever expressed this ecstasy of recognition more beautifully than Sidney Lanier in his great poem, "The Marshes of Glynn":

> As the marsh-hen secretly builds on the watery sod,
> Behold I will build me a nest on the greatness of God:
> I will fly in the greatness of God as the marsh-hen flies
> In the freedom that fills all the space twixt the marsh and
>   the skies.

So Jesus, in the first great phrase of the Lord's Prayer, sets the mood for all prayer.

CHAPTER 7

How To Pray With Love and Sacrifice

JESUS COMMANDS US TO PRAY FOR THE WORLD BEFORE WE PRAY for ourselves. He implied that He would do this in the first word of the Lord's Prayer—"Our." We are so human, our thoughts tend to revolve around I, me, mine, my aches and pains, my fears and worries, the aches and pains of my loved ones.

Jesus reminds us in "Thy Kingdom come, thy will be done on earth as it is in heaven," that our first duty as Christians is to identify ourselves with God's redemptive purpose for the world. Intercession for the needs of the world is part of the action of redemption. Our prayer for the Kingdom is the part we take with Him in helping the world to become the kind of place He wishes it to be.

Jesus not only prayed, "Thy kingdom come," He gave

His life to establish it. On the cross the whole triumph of redemptive love over man's selfishness and self-centredness was won, and that redemptive action is a living eternal thing. In the great phrase, "He ever liveth to make intercession for them" (Hebrews 7:25), we are given a picture of this continuing life of redemptive prayer.

It is as if He were saying to us: "I am alive. I am with you. When you kneel in prayer I kneel with you. And with me are the angels and archangels and all the company of heaven. We are joining our prayers to yours. Take heart, then. It is my will that love should triumph over hate, justice over injustice, right over wrong, truth over error. If I am for you, and all this great company in heaven are for you, who can be against you? Remember what I said to Martha at the tomb of Lazarus, "If thou wouldest believe, thou shouldest see the glory of God" (John 11:40).

Dr. E. Stanley Jones says, "Asking is the symbol of our desire. Some things God will not give until we want them enough to ask."[7] Our asking or intercession is the part we take with Jesus in bringing in the Kingdom. It is the highest form of creative action.

How much thought and time and discipline do we give to our prayer for others? The Roman Catholic Church considers redemptive intercession for the sins and needs of the world so important that her sons and daughters enter great praying orders like the Trappists and Carmelites and Carthusians. To these monasteries and convents go the men and women who wish to give their whole time to redemptive prayer for the world.

This is not necessary for effective prayer, however. We all can and should learn to pray as we live our daily lives.

There are several guides to effective, redemptive prayer.

The first is love and sacrifice. Love is the giving of our whole heart to a cause or a person. In redemptive prayer we give our whole heart to the cause or the person for whom we pray. We lift that cause or that person up into God's own presence in confident faith that He will supply all the needs of that cause or that person according to His great power.

Phyllis, a young college girl, did this very thing recently. One Sunday morning a long distance telephone call informed Anne, one of her friends, that her only baby niece lay dying of polio of the throat. The whole family was in a desperate state of anxiety. Phyllis' heart went out to Anne in her grief. What could she do?

She felt a strong urge to pray, so she went off to a quiet spot and poured out her soul to God for that baby. She lifted her as best she could, and placed her before God, asking for all His good gifts for her and for comfort and courage and reassurance for her family. She forgot time and place and self completely in her concern for this family.

An hour or so later, she returned to the dormitory, found Anne and two other friends, and they spent the afternoon together in quiet and prayer. Her faith and love were contagious —Anne began to come out of the state of grief and shock into which the bad news had thrown her. The other friends, both of whom had never prayed before, following Phyllis' lead, really gave themselves to prayer with her, and they began to have a confident feeling that all would be well.

At seven o'clock that night another long distance call came in. Anne went to the telephone, trembling and yet strangely at peace. Her friends stood around her in an eager circle. Her sister's voice was strong and clear at the other end.

"Anne, a miracle has happened—the doctors are amazed— the baby's throat muscles have relaxed and she is breathing normally. They say if this keeps up she will live and get well. Oh, Anne, thank God!"

Anne turned from the phone with the tears streaming down her face—tears of joy and relief—as she gave her friends the message. They couldn't say a word, they were overwhelmed, Phyllis most of all, that her small offering of love and sacrifice had produced such astounding results.

Fasting has always been considered a very important part of redemptive prayer. In this comfortable age, it is not considered good form to go to so-called extremes in anything. The practice of fasting, except occasionally on stated days or stated seasons of the church year, has not been encouraged. Yet fasting is a symbol of love and sacrifice. Jesus definitely implies this when He was able to heal the epileptic boy after His disciples had failed.

You will recall the occasion. He had just come down from the Mountain of Transfiguration, where, after fasting and deep prayer, He had suddenly been clothed with transfiguring radiance before the astonished eyes of Peter and James and John. Immediately upon descending that mountain He is faced with the challenge of the epileptic boy and the father's desperate appeal. As He heals the boy, He says simply: "This kind can come forth by nothing, but by prayer and fasting" (Mark 9:29).

If you are deeply concerned for some person or some cause I suggest that you fast and pray for a day or two. My richest experience of the results of fasting and prayer had to do with a dear friend who was going through the ordeal of watching a much loved husband slowly die of a series of strokes.

During this time I, of course, prayed daily for my friend— for courage and patience and faith for her, and for release and peace and abundant life for her husband. No assurance came to me, as it sometimes does, that he would be healed and live in this world. Neither did that assurance come to her, and one morning she experienced what so many of us go through at some time in our lives—that experience which Jesus expressed for us so heartrendingly in His blackest moment on the cross: "My God, my God, why hast thou forsaken me?" (Mark 15:34). Temporarily her faith wavered and her courage gave way. She was worn out, physically, nervously, and spiritually.

I knew at once that her desperation demanded the utmost from me. No words of mine could reach her, she was beyond human comfort. Only an extra effort of love and sacrifice on my part would help, so I fasted and prayed for her for twenty-four hours. The next morning her faith and courage had returned.

I was with her shortly afterwards when her husband died. She was quiet and steady and tender right up to the end. As we knelt at her husband's bedside she and I both felt God's divine comfort and reassurance flowing into her and sustaining her.

These two illustrations of the power of love and sacrifice need no further explanation. They carry their own message. God knows what is in our hearts. God is love and when our hearts are filled with love, they are filled with God. Then our prayers release His full love and power.

CHAPTER 8

How To Pray With Persistence

ANOTHER ESSENTIAL OF REDEMPTIVE PRAYER IS PERSISTENCE.
Many people are puzzled that Jesus put so much emphasis on
persistence in prayer. He tells us to pray without ceasing, then
he illustrates this with the stories of the unjust steward, the
laborers in the vineyard, the importunate friend and the unjust
judge. Archbishop Temple interprets these stories this way:

"We know that God does not grant petitions in order to
rid Himself of the nuisance which we become by our persistence; His choice of a parallel so completely inapposite is a
challenge to us to seek the real reason why God may make
long delay and then grant our request. . . . The purpose of
God's delay may well be to detach our faith in Him from all
trust in our own judgment. Scarcely anything deepens and
purifies faith in God for His own sake as surely as perseverance
in prayer despite long disappointment."[8]

The wonderful Old Testament story of Jacob wrestling all night with the angel is an illustration of the importance of patient persistence in prayer. You remember Jacob's final word to God as the dawn broke: "I will not let thee go, except thou bless me" (Genesis 32:26). And there He blessed Jacob.

I have been much inspired by Florence Nightingale's dogged determination to pursue what she felt was God's call to her to go into nursing. The description of her patient struggle to overcome the opposition of a neurotic mother and sister, the Victorian taboo against careers for women, the steady, jealous antagonism of the medical profession and army brass, makes challenging and inspiring reading.

From the age of seventeen, when she first felt called to nurse, until she was thirty years of age, she steadily and patiently prayed and fought for her chance. Finally, the walls of convention and prejudice crumbled before her continuous prayer. The story unfolds as if God were directing events in such a way that the skeptical world would have no choice but to yield to her fierce and obstinate will to obey God's calling to her. The results of her persistent faith were world-wide. For, in answer to prayer, God gave her the royal power to awaken the whole of society to the need for adequate, sanitary, scientific, loving care for the sick and wounded.

If we examined the lives of those who are the trail blazers of this world—the Jeanne D'Arcs, the St. Francis', the Lincolns, the Wilberforces, the Schweitzers, the Laubachs— we would see that behind their phenomenal accomplishments lies the will to pray without ceasing, "Thy kingdom come, thy will be done on earth as it is in heaven." And, "Oh, God, use me to do my small part in the building of that kingdom."

There is a new Church of the Redeemer in Greenville, South Carolina. That little church came into being in answer to the persistent prayers of seven couples. Two of the wives in this group noticed that there was no church to serve hundreds of young couples moving into a new residential area on the edge of the town. The existing church, to which these girls belonged, did not see how it could finance such a project. The rest of this story is told by Katherine Smith, the ringleader of the group. It is an eloquent illustration of the power of persistence.

"The need for a church in our end of town had been acute for ever so long, and several times at our Women's Auxiliary Chapter meetings this need had been expressed. Finally, I decided to do something about it and called seven other women to meet at my house one afternoon. After considerable discussion of ways and means, it was decided to get the co-operation of the men.

"Then a public meeting was called at the schoolhouse for all interested persons. About fifty attended that first meeting and the enthusiasm was most contagious. We got the consent of the Bishop to organize, and a vestry was elected.

"Land, or rather a suitable site, had to be found, and my husband, knowing the man who owned the finest piece of property in this locality, went to him about securing a site, but the owner did not want to sell piecemeal. We had to buy all seven acres or none at all.

"After some time had elapsed, with everybody scouring the neighborhood for a location, my prayer partner called me up and suggested that she and I would pray for the church each morning at ten o'clock, she in her house and I in mine, for nine days.

"On the ninth day, while my husband was standing on the street corner downtown, Mr. Sullivan, the owner of the property, came up to him, and said:

" 'Have you found a location for your little church? I have been thinking about you folks so much for the past few days, and I want you to have that property. I will take off the real estate commission and let you people have it for $300 less an acre. You may buy one acre this year, another acre next year, and have a five-year option on the balance until you are able to pay for it all.'

"It was truly the answer to our prayers. Exactly one year from the date of our original meeting to discuss a church we had our own priest celebrate Holy Communion, and we were an independent parish with our own budget. One year and seven months later we moved into our own building.

"From a communicant strength of approximately forty people we have more than doubled, and the church school is operating in two shifts to accommodate the children. Truly it is as if we had prayed for rain and got a cloudburst."

There are many people now meeting in small groups, linked together in daily prayer chains, with one great intention —Peace and Freedom. Some of us pray that the men in the Kremlin will repent and be converted; others that the enslaved peoples of the world will be freed; others that to the Christians behind the Iron Curtain will be given the courage and power to overcome the evil of Communist domination; others that all nations will do what is right and so earn peace.

Thousands are unitedly praying for these intentions. There should be millions. Our prayers should roll in one great swelling wave to the foot of God's throne. When He is persuaded that enough of us are serious and persistent in our concern, then He will show us through leaders whom He will guide how to establish that peace which is the fruit of righteousness.

CHAPTER 9

How To Pray in Jesus' Name

MANY PEOPLE ARE PUZZLED BY THE APPARENT CONTRADICTIONS IN Jesus' teaching on prayer. Close on the heels of His command to pray without ceasing comes the statement: "For your Father knoweth what things ye have need of before ye ask him" (Matthew 6:8). If God is omnipotent and knows what is in all our hearts, then why bother Him by telling Him what He already knows? Are we to try to change His mind? Can we persuade Him to alter the course He has charted for us or for someone else? Isn't it part of His plan that a well-rounded life must know sorrow as well as joy, struggle as well as peace, pain as well as power? I believe that Jesus solves this dilemma for us in His last great teachings on prayer in the Gospel of St. John.

And whatsoever ye shall ask in my name, that will I do, that the Father may be glorified in the Son. If ye shall ask any thing in my name, I will do it (John 14:13,14).

And in that day ye shall ask me nothing. Verily, verily, I say unto you, Whatsoever ye shall ask the Father in my name, he will give it you.

Hitherto have ye asked nothing in my name: ask and ye shall receive, that your joy may be full (John 16:23;24).

Archbishop Temple interprets these verses as follows:

"When the condition mentioned is satisfied, our wills are identified with the will of God; we are then praying for what He desires to give and wants to give until we recognize Him as its source. . . . This means that the essential act of prayer is not the bending of God's will to ours, but the bending of our wills to His. The proper outline of a Christian's prayer is not, 'Please do for me what I want' but 'Please do in me, with me and through me what you want.' "[9]

Therefore, alongside of persistence we must place trust in God's love and God's plan. We need to make our own the great assurance of St. Paul: "All things work together for good to them that love God." (Romans 8:28).

This is not the negative resignation by which we so often interpret the phrase, "Thy will be done." It means, rather, the creative, joyous confidence that in His will lie life and peace and joy, no matter how dark the immediate state of affairs.

This in fact is to pray in Jesus' name.

A simple story illustrates this great truth. A year or so ago a friend wrote to me that Mrs. N, a close fried of hers, had fled to New York to get away from a desperate personal trouble. She was praying that Mrs. N. would come and see me. A few days later, Mrs. N telephoned. She sounded like a person in deep distress. I invited her to lunch and she accepted. I found that she was a very pretty, beautifully groomed middle-aged woman, obviously well to do, but, oh, so unhappy.

Over our tea and salad, she poured out her personal tale

of woe. She had been married to an alcoholic. For years she had given up pleasure, friends, social life, in order to devote herself to helping him. In the end he had been cured of alcoholism, but not of his weakness for women.

One day he came home and calmly informed her that he was leaving her. Not a word of gratitude, appreciation, affection, or even apology. Mrs. N's whole world caved in. She felt rejected, humiliated, and bitter. She had literally fled to New York, away from the sympathy and well-intentioned advice of her friends and relatives. She had taken a hotel room, and, with the aid of sleeping pills, was nursing her grief. Her head was in a whirl, she knew no peace—what was she to do?

After she had poured it all out, I suggested that we go and kneel in the church, and pray about it. The church was dark and quiet. As we knelt there she suddenly looked up through her tears and read these words written in gold under a beautiful stained-glass window:

"In the world ye shall have tribulation, but be of good cheer, I have overcome the world" (John 16:33).

Suddenly she realized that here lay her answer. She was carrying a burden of sorrow and frustration that God wished to lift from her shoulders. Then and there, kneeling at the altar rail, she first gave Him her fear, her resentment, her sense of humiliation, and, finally, her husband. In other words, she relinquished her burden and trusted that God would fulfill His promise.

You see, Mrs. N had been demanding that God give her husband back to her; in other words, "God give me what I want." The result was the despair I have described. As we knelt at the altar she was able to say, "God, I want what you want; whether my husband and I come back together lies with you; meanwhile I will trust you fully."

It was then she began to know peace and the sense that God would lead her into happiness and usefulness and a new sense of dignity and self-respect. This He has done in abundant measure; she has become one of the most loved and creative members of her church and community. God's power to re-create her spirit, when she relinquished her burden and her will, are marvelously shown in this excerpt from one of her letters to me:

"I had been so weak that it was not at first easy to hold to my act of trust. When I first went back home, after that mountaintop experience, I found everyone wanted to discuss my trouble, sympathize and give advice. Pretty soon I felt myself slipping back into the old morass of self-pity, until I remembered that I knew what was wrong and I knew what to do. I got on my knees and talked it out with God.

"I said: 'Dear God, I have given this all to you. Let your will be done in the lives of both of us. You know what is best.'

"The sense of release came back and this time it was so complete. One day I was sitting on the lawn and I realized that I wasn't worried any more—it was all gone—no wrong feelings left—no resentment—no bitterness, self-pity or any of the things that wreck us.

"Now I don't worry. I live one day at a time. I give the day to God in the morning and thank Him at night for all He has done that day. I have also learned to stop and give things to God as they come, no matter how little they are. Giving the little things to Him all along makes it so easy to take the big things to Him too. Isn't it wonderful?

"I have been able to help my son at a time when he needed it. God just laid the right book in my hands to help him. It was given to me the day before he came and I knew it was the answer when he called me. I sat and wrote, in the front and back of it, the things that had helped me most and it was so good to be able to say, 'Oh, darling, these are not things I have just read or heard, but things I have tried and I know what they will do. You know what God has done for me and if you will honestly give everything to Him He will do the same thing for you.' Everything is so right for him now and you know how happy this makes me.

"I do want the love of God that I feel, and the peace of mind I have, for every man, woman and child. It is such a wonderful way to live. My heart is full of praise to Him."

This happened two years ago. Recently I met Mrs. N at a gathering in New York and did not recognize her at first—every line in her face had changed. This smiling, radiant woman was the same Mrs. N and yet how different, because God had restored her soul.

Mrs. N had not only learned to live her life God's way, but she had learned to pray in His name. That is real prayer. Through it we help to restore the world to God. He is the Master Weaver. He has created a glorious design for this world as the great tapestry designers did in the Middle Ages, but He depends on us, His people, to follow His design as He has outlined it on His drawing board.

We weave the tapestry with the threads of praise, persistence, trust, love, and sacrifice. Like the ancient weavers, we weave from behind, obediently following directions on His blueprint, and as we weave, the great design takes shape and gradually stands out clear and complete. It can happen to us; it can happen to others through us; it can happen to our world—if we trust Him and pray in His name.

CHAPTER 10

How To Ask For Forgiveness

ONE CONDITION OF ALL POWERFUL PRAYER IS EMPHASIZED BY THE phrase, "Forgive us our trespasses as we forgive those who trespass against us." Unless our attitude toward God is repentant He won't hear us. Unless our attitude toward others is forgiving and redemptive, He won't hear us.

It is no accident that the Church sets aside forty days each year for fasting, penitence and prayer in order that we may examine ourselves and prepare our hearts and minds for the glorious experience of Easter. Jesus' forty days in the wilderness were just such a time of self-purification.

So with us. God has given us the gift of prayer. Prayer is spiritual dynamite. We cannot use it to satisfy self-interest and personal ambition or merely human desire. We need a constant cleansing of our inner attitudes.

Recently a friend asked this alarming question of a group of self-complacent Christians. "How would you like to remain in the room if all your thoughts were projected on a silver screen with the title: 'One Hour in The Thought Life of Helen Smith Shoemaker, or Mary A. Randolph, or Priscilla B. Yates'?" We laughed, but our mirth was uneasy.

In the Book of Common Prayer there is a prayer called the "General Confession." This prayer is said in preparation for Holy Communion. It is a very disquieting prayer. We say this:

"Almighty God, Father of our Lord Jesus Christ, Maker of all things, Judge of all men; we acknowledge and bewail our manifold sins and wickedness, which we, from time to time, most grievously have committed by thought, word and deed, against thy Divine Majesty, provoking most justly thy wrath and indignation against us. We do earnestly repent, and are heartily sorry for these our misdoings; the remembrance of them is grievous unto us; the burden of them is intolerable. Have mercy upon us, have mercy upon us, most merciful Father; For thy Son our Lord Jesus Christ's sake, forgive us all that is past; and grant that we may ever hereafter serve and please thee in newness of life, To the honour and glory of thy Name; through Jesus Christ our Lord. Amen" (Anglican Book of Common Prayer).

Many people say to me, "I don't like to say the General Confession, because I really don't feel it necessary to 'bewail my manifold sins and wickedness.' I do not feel very sinful or very wicked. I do not grievously commit sin 'by thought, word and deed against His Divine Majesty.' I don't really believe that I 'provoke his wrath and his indignation against me.'"

If a poll were taken, most of us would agree that the General Confession is overdone, the language too archaic for modern Christians. It all seems an exaggeration. We have been going to church, many of us all our lives; we have been saying our prayers regularly, we have been trying to live by the Golden Rule, we are neighborly and big-hearted, and generous. We are conscientious wives, husbands, parents; we are trying to be honest in business. How, then, does it apply to us?

It applies to us very directly if we identify ourselves with all Christian people. When we think of saying the General Confession for the Christian people in the world, as well as for ourselves, and taking our share of the blame for the compromise in the Christian Church, it puts matters in a very different light. As we look at the world around us we cannot be very proud of what we members of the Christian Church have accomplished in bringing in the Kingdom for which we pray every time we say the Lord's Prayer.

As one very great Latvian Christian said to some of us a short time ago, "Twenty million Communists are taking the world away from six hundred million Christians." There are only twenty million really dedicated Communists on the party rolls of the Communist party, and there are six hundred million enrolled Christians.

When we look at the corruption in public life—both state and national—when we look at the racial and national prejudice still rampant in the world, when we consider the very unpleasant fact that one out of every twelve people in the United States is either neurotic or emotionally or mentally confused, it doesn't make us feel very effective as Christians, does it? If we were more vital, if we were more dedicated, if we were really channels of God's holy power and energy, these conditions would not continue to exist, and Communism would have no appeal. Communism has no appeal to people who are well fed, both physically and spiritually. Communism appeals to the physically and spiritually starved. If the Christian Church were a pillar of fire leading the peoples of the world, instead of an ambulance corps, bringing up the rear as it so often seems to be, Communism probably would not have been born.

Someone recently put into my hands a little pamphlet by Agnes Sanford, the well-known writer and healer. She says this about the need for the repentance of Christians:

"There is an answer to the crisis of this hour. There is a power greater than the power of the atom bomb, that can swing the course of history into the paths of peace. But we, God's people, who are called by His name, have blocked this power. So now, when we try to pray for the world, only one answer comes to us: 'Repent. If my people who are called by my name shall humble themselves and pray and seek my face and turn from their wicked ways, then will I hear from heaven and will forgive their sin and will heal their land.'

"God is able to heal our land, His power is unlimited, His resources infinite, the history of His people is full of times when in answer to the prayer of repentance He has intervened directly in the affairs of men and of nations, and has saved His people by guidance and inspiration, and even by the forces of nature, wind and fog and water and fire. He has reserves of spiritual energy locked up in the spirits of men as physical energy is locked up in the atom. Who knows how many Pentecosts there could be today with the world full of those who try to pray, if only we take the necessary step of discarding our sins, personal and national, so as to get through to the center of power."[10]

So much for our share in the guilt of all of us as a so-called Christian nation. What about our personal guilt? What about our personal sin? A great many of the things that we consider sin are the result of partial commitment, partial trust, partial dedication. We are always hoeing and scraping our souls for the little things, such as, "I was selfish yesterday," or "I lost my temper," or "I have gossiped about my mother-in-law," or "I was rude to so-and-so," when our real trouble is much deeper.

Gossip, criticism, pride, intolerance, prejudice, hatreds—these are the symptoms of sin, not sin itself. If sin is anything that keeps us from God or another person it shows itself in all these reactions. It does not matter whether we are in church every time the doors open, or whether we are good, faithful church workers; the Pharisees did all these things and yet Jesus reserved His most scathing denunciation for them.

One symptom of a half dedicated life is self-centredness, touchiness and credit-snatching. I meet women constantly who are unhappy in their church group. They say that the other women in the church are cold and snobbish or try to wall off our newcomers. They feel lonesome and insecure and un-wanted. Often they either continue to come with a chip on their shoulders or leave and go to another church, only to discover that the same conditions exist there. Or they stop going to church altogether, stating as their reason that the church is so full of hypocrites that they cannot be bothered with it.

What these people need to do is to search their own souls to see if the fault does not lie partly in themselves. The church has never claimed to be a society of saints, but rather a fellowship of sinners, each of us imperfect but each of us trying to pattern his life more nearly on His whom we come to church to worship.

One of my friends who was unhappy in her church

took herself in hand and decided to check herself by the words of Jesus when He said, "Take heed to yourselves." She found that when she relinquished her own hostility and antagonism she began to feel better. Further, she concentrated on trying to please God and serving Him wholeheartedly.

She then started to pray for the people who had hurt her. It came to her that God had created them as well as herself, therefore He must love them as much as He loved her, and she sincerely hoped He loved her. Quite to her surprise, she had no longer felt snubbed when she attended a parish dinner or a circle meeting. It wasn't long before she began to love and admire the very women who had seemed so formidable. You see, in prayer she rediscovered a very old secret—self-centredness and touchiness act like a boomerang. They set up a negative situation in the persons whom we fear or dislike, and they become antagonistic.

My friend had been thinking of the church as a social club, not as a fellowship of men and women dedicated to a living Lord. When she put first things first she was able to see those around her through Christ's eyes, and in those eyes there was only understanding and compassion.

Another symptom of a half-dedicated heart and soul is prejudice. Many of us feel that because we are Episcopalians or Baptists, or Roman Catholics, that, somehow, we are superior to all other Christians. Others of us feel that because we are Christians we are superior to Jews, or because we are white we are superior to blacks.

I had this brought home to me very forcibly on my return from a visit to Texas. My train stopped in St. Louis, and I got out for an hour. As I went through the station gate to get into my car again, I noticed a very handsome dark-skinned boy standing at the gate. I didn't know whether he was a Negro or an Indian, so I decided to find out. I asked, "Are you from India? I have many friends in India, and you look like an Indian."

He replied in broken English, "No, I am from the West Indies."

As I passed on I noticed that he came through the gate and got into my car. A white man was seeing him off, and he looked lonely, so I made up my mind I would make friends with him. As soon as the train got under way, I went to his little compartment. In what I thought was my most gracious tone of voice I said, "How do you do again." He looked at me blankly.

I had an inspiration. I said, *Vous parlez français, alors?* At which his face lit up and he beamed with pleasure. *Ah, oui, je parle français, madame.* So I went ahead with my rather bad French, and he replied in his very good French.

We had a grand time, but he would interrupt himself to say, *Mais je n'aime pas Les Etats Unis* ("I do not like the United States"). I was a bit taken aback, as it seemed a rude way to repay my courtesy, but I sensed that something lay behind his attitude, and gradually I drew the story out of him.

He was a member of one of the best families in his country. His father owned a book business in the capital city. The boy was making his first visit to the United States. It was unfortunate that he should have entered a part of the country where segregation is practiced. He had come to St. Louis to visit a publishing house for his father. There he ran into segregation in attempting to find a hotel in which to stay. The white publisher explained to the manager of the hotel that the boy was a distinguished foreigner and he was accepted, but the incident left a scar.

He was briefed not to speak any English while in certain

parts of the United States in order to avoid further un-
pleasantness. The boy wondered resentfully how this squared
with the "land of the free," as he had heard the United
States described. However, he took his friend's advice and
decided he would pretend not to know English. That is why
he looked blank when I came to his compartment door.

After a long and happy conversation, I invited him to
take lunch with me in the dining car. He looked at me
oddly, but accepted. So I took him in to luncheon, and as
he got near the dining car he said, *Madame, est-ce que je peux
entrer ici?* ("Madame, may I come in here?")

I said, "Certainly, you may come in here; you come with
me." We sat down, as it happened, opposite a couple of men.
I thought to myself, rather wickedly, "This is going to be
fun." As I introduced him to the men, I said, "You know, this
young man is from the West Indies."

Well, these men, who had looked very much disturbed
when we entered, began to try to be gracious. I could almost
watch them rationalize. "We don't mind eating with this
young man; true he's colored but he is different because he
is from the West Indies."

Meanwhile, my friend was still looking agitated, and as
we began to eat, he looked out of the window and said suddenly, in French, "What state are we in now?" I said, "We
are in Indiana." He said, "Is that the North?" I said, "Yes,
we are in the North." "Oh," he said, "then I can speak
English."

This story has elements of humor, but underneath there
is something deeply wrong when a young colored man's first
exposure to the United States should have made such an
unfortunate impression. I couldn't help wondering about the
report he would carry back to his counrty of the way in

which we behave to Negro or colored visitors. Many South Americans are very dark-skinned, some a mixture of Negro, Spanish, or Portuguese blood.

I wonder how our race prejudice affects our good-neighbor efforts in Central and South America or in Asia and Africa. How dangerous for us that we, a Christian people, should allow such conditions to exist in our country!

"Every act of racial discrimination or prejudice in the United States is blown up by the Communists abroad, and it hurts America as much as an espionage agent who turns over a weapon to a foreign enemy. Every American citizen can contribute toward creating a better understanding of American ideals abroad by practicing and thinking tolerance and respect for human rights every day of the year." So said Vice-President Richard Nixon on his return from a state visit to Asia.

I have mentioned several symptoms of a partially dedicated life, national complacence, self-centredness, and prejudice. Search your own soul for the others and put pride, both national and personal, at the top of the list. Then get down on your knees and ask God to forgive you. When you have done this, offer your prayers and He will hear you.

CHAPTER 11

How To Pray For Those Who Sin Against Society

LET US NOW TURN FROM "FORGIVE US OUR TRESPASSES" TO THE other side of the coin, "as we forgive those who trespass against us."

Peter came to Jesus and said, "Lord, how oft shall my brother sin against me and I forgive him? till seven times?" Jesus replied, "I say not unto thee, Until seven times; but, Until seventy times seven" (Matthew 18:21;22). Earlier He had told His disciples, "For if ye forgive men their trespasses, your heavenly Father will also forgive you. But if ye forgive not men their trespasses, neither will your Father forgive your trespasses" (Matthew 6:14;15).

One of my audience at a school of prayer was very much disturbed by this statement. It sounded like tit for tat to her. She didn't think God was a revengeful God. We had a long conversation about it. He is not a revengeful God, but when we refuse to forgive our brother his trespasses, we block the stream of His power. We set up a barrier between ourselves and God so that His power cannot flow towards us. We do this, He does not. He does not revenge Himself—He is not that kind of a God. He merely allows us to cut ourselves off from Him by our wrong attitudes.

There is a legend that Leonardo da Vinci, when painting "The Last Supper," painted the head of his enemy on the shoulders of Judas. That night he could not sleep. The following day he was to paint the head of Christ, but every time he tried to see the face it blurred. So after another sleepless night he got up, went to his studio and erased the head of his enemy from the shoulders of Judas. Immediately he saw the head of Christ clearly.

There are three attitudes that we can take toward those who have sinned against us and those who have sinned against society. We can condemn them, we can condone their sins, or we can redeem them.

One can easily see that condemning does not get either those we condemn or ourselves anywhere. It leaves us sitting in a nice little pool of self-righteousness. It bars them out of our prayers and out of our lives. Neither does condoning get them or us anywhere. That is too sentimental.

"Forgiveness is not supine," runs a quotation. "It is a beneficent invasion. It is alert and patient and creative."

Our forgiveness of others must be like God's forgiveness of us. He has so much to forgive us. He is so gracious and patient with us that we can hardly be less alert, patient, and creative toward those who have wronged us.

First, shall we apply this principle to those who have sinned against society? How shall we pray for them? We can condemn them. If we do, we cannot pray for them. We can condone them and excuse their sin, or we can redeem them through prayer. Our prayers can become the beneficent invasion which seeks to draw them away from their wrong attitudes and actions into the ways of God once more. Justice demands that the Hitlers and Stalins of the world pay the penalty for their deeds, but mercy seeks to redeem their hearts and souls. Is that, perhaps, the proper attitude to take?

In an article in the *Saturday Evening Post* a Lutheran chaplain assigned by the United States Army to the Nazi war criminals during their trial in Nurnberg reports that being a Christian, he knew that if the thief on the cross could repent and be redeemed in his death agony, it was possible that even a Nazi war criminal might repent and die in a state of grace. So the chaplain offered himself as God's channel to these men and because of his redemptive love he won the confidence of even the most hardened. With one or two exceptions, they made confession and received absolution before their deaths. Justice demanded that they pay the full penalty required by international law for their crimes against society, but because one man's prayers and one man's attitudes were completely redemptive God used him to seek and save that which was lost.[11]

The story of this chaplain's action has helped me in my attitude towards the leaders of the Kremlin. For a long time I could not pray for them. I felt that their crimes against humanity and against God had been too great for them to deserve the notice of any decent person's prayers. Then I remembered that they were lost souls if ever there were any. If Jesus came to seek and to save the lost, could I, His follower, do less?

Several times I have attended funerals of people who

have broken every rule in the book—men and women who have been belligerent agnostics, alcoholics, libertines—unrepentant to the end. Their loving relatives have seen to it that they had beautiful Christian funerals. I often wondered how the minister could read the glorious words of the funeral service with any sincerity for such people, and yet he does. When he comes to that tremendous passage, which I have already mentioned in this book—the last passage in the eighth chapter of St. Paul's Epistle to the Romans, one suddenly understands.

For I am persuaded that neither death, nor life, nor angels, nor principalities, nor powers, nor things present, nor things to come, nor height, nor depth, nor any other creature, shall be able to separate us from the love of God, which is in Christ Jesus our Lord (Romans 8:37).

So that is it. No matter what we do or do not do, God never gives us up. His love follows us into this world and through our lives and into the next world. We can repudiate Him and break His laws and hurt our fellow men and ruin our own lives and still He loves us, not sentimentally, tepidly or supinely, but with a strength that in the end will not be denied.

We cannot flee Him, the Hitlers and Stalins cannot flee Him. He will catch up with us all some day, somewhere, and we will turn and fall on our knees before Him. Yes, even the Hitlers and Stalins will receive the opportunity to turn and fall on their knees before Him; for He is God and God is love.

There is a sin mentioned in the Gospels and the Epistles, the sin against the Holy Spirit, which we are told will not be forgiven. What that sin is, is shrouded in mystery. It may be the denial of God; it may be such repeated flouting of His great law of love that the man or woman who does it is consigned to perpetual outer darkness. It is not for us to judge this! "Vengeance is mine; I will repay," saith the Lord (Romans 12:19). It is for us to throw our prayers into the breach wherever there is a chance that a soul may be salvaged by them.

Thus it is possible to pray for a Stalin, for who knows but that a prayer we pray may open a crack in the hard cement of such a sinner's heart.

CHAPTER 12

How To Pray For Those Who Sin Against Us

IT IS EASIER TO PRAY FOR THOSE WHO HAVE SINNED AGAINST society than for those who have sinned against us personally. I doubt that there is a single individual reading this book who has not been sinned against, or does not feel that he or she has been sinned against by someone. What are we to do about these people who have sinned against us? Are we going to try to avoid them—wall them out of our thinking and our lives? That may be possible, but it is no solution. What if one of these people lives in the same house with us?

There are thousands of mothers with rebellious children, thousands of wives with unfaithful husbands, thousands of children with problem parents.

I know a widow who has laid down her life for her son.

She has refused remarriage, she has earned the money to put her son through school and college. She has loved and nurtured him with great care and great self-sacrifice.

Apparently the boy has not appreciated all this. He rebelled, and at the first opportunity he left her and went off on his own. He has not attempted to repay her or support her in any way for all the years of self-giving. What is the mother to do? She can condemn, or she can condone his conduct, or she can redeem this son. She has chosen the third course.

First, she has examined herself to see where she may have failed, and she has discovered possessiveness and a demand for appreciation and thanks which she sees put an emotional pressure on her boy which he could not or would not meet. Then she discovered self-pity and "How could he be so cruel to me?" attitudes in herself. Lastly, she found that she had indulged and protected him throughout his childhood so that he was not equipped, either emotionally or spiritually, to meet her demands.

This woman is a brave woman. She has faced her own faults in this relationship and asked forgiveness for them. She has not blamed or resented the boy's conduct, rather she has put him into God's hands, patiently praying and believing that he will find God's plan for his life and his future. Meanwhile, she is continuing cheerfully to earn her own living and make her own life. That is living and praying redemptively.

Through the years I have watched one of my closest friends restore an unstable, alcoholic husband to normalcy. She has patiently stood by him through the temperamental instabilities of his early effort to break the habit. She has given up her own very successful career in order to further his. She has sought in every way possible to create the kind of relaxed, beautiful home to which he would want to return. He has been irritable and rebellious, self-centred in turn, but her love has held firm and her confident faith that he would find the way has triumphed over every set-back. He has found the way and become not only a good husband but a successful member of society.

We hear a great deal today about prodigal parents and I have been amazed at the patience, long-suffering and maturity of some people's children.

I have a young friend who illustrates perfectly the difference between condemning, condoning, and redeeming, a very difficult family situation in which she was caught. When she was very young her father divorced her mother. The child was given into his custody. A year later he married another woman. The other woman decided to show the world she could bring this child up as a lady. Her pattern of behavior was to treat her very much as the stepmother treated Cinderella. She was not allowed to go out in the evening, not allowed lipstick or pretty clothes; onerous household chores were given her.

The only matter the stepmother could not control was the child's love for the church and her desire to go there. It was undoubtedly God's love and power that the girl experienced in the church fellowship that gave her the steadiness to remain alert and patient and creative in the midst of her personal ordeal.

When she was seventeen her father's eye began to wander once more, and, to add to the girl's troubles the stepmother went to pieces emotionally. After a time of prayer, Diana knew the time had come to challenge her father. She hated to hurt him, as she loved him, but she realized that if she could prevent it she could not allow him to disrupt any more lives.

So she gathered her courage and went to his office. She talked to him straight from the shoulder. He denied everything, but she countered with, "Daddy, I am sorry, but I know what you are doing. You helped to wreck one home and now you are preparing to wreck another. For all our sakes you will have to change your ways." It was very direct, very simple, very loving. There was something about her—God in her perhaps—that the father could not deny. After a time of great turmoil and conflict, he came around. He and the stepmother were reconciled.

God's reward to this wonderful child was the rediscovery of her own mother. She had been kept away from her mother. It was probably just as well, for during the eight or ten years when she did not see her mother, the latter, who had been a very weak and self-indulgent woman, got hold of herself, repented of her shortcomings, and found a rich, strong faith of her own.

It may have been due to Diana's believing prayers, for during those years of separation she told me that her love and prayers and yearning for her own mother grew steadily stronger. The moment she was of age she went and found her mother again. Their reunion must have been very touching, for she wrote about it so joyfully:

"Mother's been finding what I have been finding, possibly as a result of our prayers, and the wonder of it is that our two hearts have met in a greater love."

I met a woman last summer who had one of the saddest faces I have ever seen. She was a widow. She had been widowed for some time. One day she asked if she might talk with me. After some preliminaries, she burst out with,

"You know, I simply can't get out of my heart my hatred for the man who I feel was the cause of my husband's death. My husband knew that he was both dishonest and irresponsible, but he hoped to change him by kindness and patience. The strain and anxiety of the whole situation caused the stroke that killed my husband. I cannot shake off my hatred for this man. I used to be interested in the church and all kinds of civic affairs, but I can't concentrate on anything any more. Nothing interests me—I feel so lost and desperate."

We talked a long time. I told her about the many imaginary conversations I had held with myself about other people, wanting to get even, wanting to give blow for blow, wanting to have the last word, until I realized that how other people behaved to me was not my business but God's. My only concern was to forgive others as God forgave me.

Finally she realized that she was only injuring herself by harboring these feelings of resentment. Very reluctantly she relinquished her idea of how this man should be punished. She put him in God's hands, and trusted him to God's justice. During the next few days a slow transformation took place. She began to look less sad and preoccupied. Ways in which she could again take up her interests and serve in her town began to come to her.

"It's such a relief to discover that I am not responsible for the punishment of this man," she said to me. "I don't feel any more as though I could never speak to him again. I can actually bring him into God's light in prayer, and pray that in that light he will see light. I felt so far away from my husband while these bitter thoughts possessed me; now I feel close to him again, for he never held bitter thoughts, and I'm sure he is still trying to reach that man's heart from the other world. Can I do less?"

These are inspiring stories of the way in which one can act in a nearly impossible situation, a situation in which one has had every excuse to be resentful and unforgiving.

The most difficult people to forgive are the people who resist us, those who resist our will. Have you ever felt frustrated and angered by somebody who continually resists you?

For instance, if you are religious, if you believe in saying your prayers, if you like to go to church, and your husband or your child or your mother or your father does not, what do you do? Many people come to me and say, "I'm just boiling with resentment. I can't get my husband to say his prayers or go to church. He won't do anything I want. Wouldn't you think he might do it to please me?"

One of the worst sins of wives (being a wife myself) is wanting our husbands to find their way to the Lord our way, exactly our way, and to persist in tugging them along like lagging children. Many women have complained to me about this and I reply, "Pray for your husband and really live like a Christian at home, and let him grow his wings his way. One day he will come to church on his own initiative." This has happened in instance after instance in which the wife has surrendered her willfulness.

Do you have trouble forgiving yourself? Over and over and over do you blame yourself? If you do, try to remember that God loves you, that God loves you much more than He judges you. He tries to bring us to see our sins, yes, our failures, the things we do to put up barriers between ourselves and other people and Him. But the most important thing about God is that He loves us. He is not trying to punish us. He is trying to draw us to Him, so that He can use us as His channels. We block the channel when we fill it with self-blame and inferiority and continual self-scrutiny. We must trust ourselves to God's love as we trust ourselves to the water when learning to swim. Just as we cannot learn to swim if we thrash and struggle in the water, so we can never learn the greatness of God's love unless we take Jesus' word and trust ourselves to Him.

A woman of my acquaintance has a daughter who has miserably failed as wife and mother. She is weak, self-indulgent, and self-centred. The mother has been overcome with self-blame and an overwhelming sense of failure and guilt. She is not helping her child by taking this attitude. She has been a woman of real Christian faith, but has allowed her sense of guilt and self-blame to become obsessive to the point where it is like a black cloud blotting out the sun. Her friends, through their care and prayers, are trying to help her back to a sense of God's love and forgiveness so that once more she may stand strong in hope and faith rather than in self-doubt and despair.

Finally, there are those of us who need to forgive God. How many there are who, under the shock of great personal tragedy, turn from God and His Church with the bitter words, "Why has this happened to me? What have I done to deserve this?" When we do this we retreat from every possibility of healing or comfort. In our self-centred grief we reject the verdict of history, of the millions of people who have put their hands into the hand of God when it was night so that He might lead them into the dawn.

One day last winter, after a talk on forgiveness, a lovely looking woman came up to me. She said, "The last thing you said about 'forgiving God' struck me. My son, a pilot, has been missing in Korea since Christmas. I asked God bitterly, 'Why should it be my son?' and He gave me an assurance which dispelled my bitterness and has stayed with me through all these months, that wherever Kim is, he is in his Father's keeping and is fulfilling his destiny. I just know that God is watching over and using Kim. I wish I could share this assurance with all the bitter, grieving mothers."

Prayer is the ladder we build to heaven. Our intercessions ascend and His blessings descend. If any rung of that ladder is faulty we shall miss our step, and our prayers cannot ascend. That is why Jesus placed at the very heart of His perfect prayer this key: "Forgive us our trespasses as we forgive those who trespass against us."

CHAPTER 13

How God Guides Us

WE MODERN CHRISTIANS NEED TO RECAPTURE THE VIVID SENSE of the Living Presence of Christ in the person of His Holy Spirit. The early disciples took Jesus' promises about the Holy Spirit in St. John's Gospel quite literally. The first ten chapters of the Book of Acts is a vivid record of how God, through His Holy Spirit, guided the first Christians in establishing Christianity in the Roman world.

What did Jesus tell us about the Holy Spirit? Some church leaders feel that a comma should be placed after "Lead us" in that phrase of the Lord's prayer, "Lead us, not into temptation." They say that Jesus intends to refer to the guiding power of the Holy Spirit. One ancient version of the Lord's Prayer puts it this way, "Lead us, lest we fall into temptation."

Jesus is very specific in describing the rôle of the Holy

78

Spirit. First, the Holy Spirit is to be a counselor. Second, He will make the truth plain and give courage to follow it. Third, He will be in us. Fourth, He will teach us. Fifth, He will remind us of Jesus' teaching and His commands. Sixth, He will guide us and give us foresight. Seventh, He will give us power.

So, in a nutshell, Jesus introduces us to the Holy Spirit. The doctrine of the Holy Spirit tells us that God is very close to us—nearer to us than breathing, closer than hands or feet. Therefore, He is continually seeking to communicate with us. "Only because it is God's nature to reveal or communicate Himself is there a world at all. Everything in it, every single occurrence in time or space, is subject to this controlling fact, that the world exists as the arena of God's self-revelation."[12]

God revealed Himself in all His glory to us in the person of Jesus. He is still seeking to reveal Himself to us through the Holy Spirit, who is the Living Spirit of Christ.

In the *Conversion of the Church,* by S. M. Shoemaker, the author reminds us of the central importance of listening for the guidance of the Holy Spirit. He says, "Religion today is largely the imitation of an example when it ought to be the hearing of a voice. And so the interior life of Christians has become a dynamo, busy with plans and philanthropies and activities, when it ought to be a receiving set primarily concerned with catching the messages from on high." Does that fit any of us?

To a person puzzled about the whole question of Divine guidance a humorous British friend wrote a postcard. On it he drew a man's face with two big ears and a small mouth. Underneath he wrote, "You have two ears and a small mouth. Why don't you listen twice as much as you talk?"

Whether it be in personal prayer, or group prayer, or even

in our great services of public worship, a time should be set aside for silence and listening. When we telephone a friend we do not do all the talking and then replace the receiver before listening for his reply. Prayer is not a one-way street. We do not travel up it to a dead end. No, in prayer we go up the street to meet God and He comes down the street to meet us. Out of that meeting and the counsel and direction He gives us comes our action in building His Kingdom.

There is a story that one day an Episcopalian was invited to a Quaker meeting. The congregation sat together in silence so long that the Episcopalian grew restless and whispered to his Quaker friend, "When does the service begin?" To which the Quaker replied, "The service begins when the meeting ends." This may be the secret of the extraordinary effectiveness of the rather small Quaker group. They wait together in silence until the inner light of the Holy Spirit illuminates them unitedly, then they act with power.

In the tenth chapter of the Book of Acts is told the story of how the Holy Spirit, through guiding two men, changed the course of history. One of the men was a Roman centurion. Apparently this man, like many Romans, had been profoundly affected by the Jewish belief in one God. He prayed to God as the Jews prayed, and one day as he was praying for more understanding God's Holy Spirit came to him in a vision and told him to send his servants to Joppa and find a man called Peter, who would enlighten him further. The Roman did not question his vision, as we are so apt to do. He obeyed and immediately sent his servants on their errand.

The other man was St. Peter. St. Peter was praying on the housetop of a friend and he saw a vision of a great sheet let down from heaven and in it all manner of creeping things and four-footed beasts. A voice said: "Rise, Peter; kill and eat."

Peter was not as quick in his obedience as the centurion. He questioned the validity of the vision. All his Jewish training and prejudice rose up in resistance. No pious Jew would consider eating any meat that was not kosher. It was considered mortal sin. Again the voice said: "What God hath cleansed, that call not thou common." Peter was not yet convinced. He was not sure that this might not be a temptation. Possibly he recalled the phrase in the Lord's Prayer, "Lead us not into temptation," and hesitated lest this be false guidance. As Peter hesitated, the three servants of Cornelius knocked on the door of the house and asked for him. While they were knocking the Holy Spirit spoke to Peter again: "Behold, three men seek thee. Arise, therefore, and get thee down, and go with them, doubting nothing; for I have sent them."

Peter stopped questioning and obeyed. The men took him to Cornelius' house. Cornelius had invited all his friends and relatives to meet and hear Peter. You see Cornelius was so sure Peter would come that he was all ready. Peter, introducing himself, told them how unlawful it was for a good Jew to meet, or associate in any way with, non-Jews. "But," he concluded with amazement, "God hath shewed me that I should not call any man common or unclean." He proceeded to tell them all about Jesus, and as he reached the climax of his story, the whole company was visited with a united sense of the presence of the Holy Spirit.

This story illustrates perfectly the sevenfold action of the Holy Spirit. He counseled with Cornelius and Peter as they prayed. He sent an angel to speak with Cornelius and appeared in a dream to Peter. He made the truth plain to Peter in his dream. He gave both men the courage to obey His guidance. He filled Peter with grace and wisdom as he spoke to Cornelius and his friends. He reminded Peter to tell them of Jesus' teaching. He gave Peter foresight in his dream. He released His power into the whole company when Peter had done speaking.

This event, perhaps more than any other in history, marks the establishment of the Christian Church in the world. If Cornelius had not obeyed, the good news about Jesus might not have been carried to the pagan world. If Peter had not obeyed, it is quite possible that Christianity would have remained a Jewish sect. There was a very real chance that Peter's intolerance and prejudice—the result of the traditional exclusiveness of the Jewish people—might have overruled the guidance of the Holy Spirit.

It is startling to us to realize that the course of history was changed by two men's obedience to guidance. It is still more startling to us to realize that the building of Christ's Kingdom often depends on just such obedience.

This great truth was put to me very simply years ago. "God has a plan. You have a part. Find it. Follow it." How wonderful that each of us can have a part in carrying out God's plan. Unless we learn to listen for the guidance of His Holy Spirit and obey Him, we will miss our part.

Possibly that is what is wrong with the world. So many people miss their parts. Either through indifference or unbelief, or just plain sin. That is the reason why prayer is so vitally important. It helps the people for whom we pray to find God's way and their part in it. It also helps us to find God's way and our part in it.

Recently in a small Midwestern town, under pressure of a near tragedy, a whole group of formerly unrelated people were brought together under the guidance of the Holy Spirit, and the result was a miracle. I have the story from one of the heroines. Here is the story:

We live in a friendly little town. For the past year or more three or four couples of us have met each Sunday evening for prayer. One morning I was called to the phone and it was the business manager of the hospital, one of our prayer partners, to say a young mother had just been admitted to the hospital. We knew her, oh, so well. The parents and grandparents had been active in business and church and were liked by the whole community. In the family were three children, one under a year old.

That morning, when the sister, Mary, called and asked the little boy for his mother he said, "She can't come to the phone, she is lying on the floor upstairs." Mary rushed over to their home. She discovered that Katharine had had a cerebral hemorrhage.

When the word came to me that morning, I called those closest to Katharine and prayer started. There was no particular planning. That evening at seven we met at the church and lifted our voices and our hearts to God, giving our young friend into His care, praying for the husband, the parents, the sister, and the little children, as well as those who were caring for them.

The news spread through the town like a prairie fire. There was prayer for Katharine when the choir met for practice, there was prayer for her at the Parent Teachers meeting. Each evening a group met in the church, and people hearing of it asked to be allowed to join the group.

Katharine's left side was paralyzed. We were told that if she lived three days there might be hope for her recovery. The three days passed. Our prayers continued.

The doctors knew that the only way to save her life would be to remove the clot, but until there was consciousness the operation could not be performed. So we prayed some more. Then came flashes of consciousness and a bit of movement on the left side.

The time had come, but the brain surgeon was one hundred miles away. Could she possibly live through such a hazardous journey? The doctor and her family decided to risk it. The day that she was moved, we prayed all day long, dividing the time into half-hour periods. Katharine's own Methodist friends, as well as Roman Catholics, Christian Scientists, and members of the Church of God, joined in this prayer chain.

Our prayers were heard. The trip was made with no ill effects. This operation takes from six to sixteen hours. Careful preparation has to be made, the right anesthetist is most important. Soon word came back that the operation would be Thursday at one o'clock.

Again the half-hour prayer periods were taken. I was at prayer between five-thirty and six. I had a strong sense of urgency to uphold the doctor and the anesthetist particularly.

At seven o'clock we heard that Katharine had survived the operation; it was successful. We were assured that if she lived through the first three post-operative days her convalescence would be normal. There were moments when it did not seem that she could make it. Our prayers continued.

Then one morning when her husband went into her room she said, "Hi," completely conscious. It was not long before she was up on her feet, then she was walking a few steps, then returning home.

This has been a tremendous testimony to our church and our town of the power of prayer. It frightens me to think of the many others who should be upheld by consistent prayer, whom we have failed because we have been too busy, or have not cared enough.

This drama highlights the phrase I used in introducing the story, "God has a plan, you have a part, find it, follow it."

The near tragedy of the young mother enlisted the sympathetic action of a number of people. One of these people, however, was a woman who believed deeply in prayer and because she believed this, she was open to discovering how to pray and act most effectively in this crisis. Her part was to mobilize the prayer power of a whole town in behalf of Katharine and because she did this, courage, wisdom, love and power were released in and through the other actors in the drama that brought about what might be called a "miracle."

Ordinary people were strengthened and encouraged to do extraordinary things. A new "energy" was let loose in that "friendly little town."

This can happen in your town, it can happen in your block, it can happen in your family—if you learn to listen for and then obey the guidance of the Holy Spirit.

CHAPTER 14

How Prayer Helps The Sick

DR. NORMAN VINCENT PEALE SAYS THIS ABOUT CREATIVE PRAYER:

Personally, I believe that prayer is a sending out of vibrations from one person to another and to God. All the universe is in vibration. There are vibrations in the molecules of a table. The air is filled with vibrations. The reaction between human beings is also vibration. When you send out a prayer for another person, you employ the force inherent in a spiritual universe. You transport from yourself to the other person a sense of love, helpfulness, support—a sympathetic, powerful understanding—and in this process you awaken vibrations in the universe through which God brings to pass the good objectives prayed for.[13]

A well-known writer on atomic science, the late Dr. John O'Neill, told a group of church people, of which I was one, that many atomic scientists—through purely scientific experiment—had come to the conclusion that all energy was vested in the Godhead. Atomic energy was merely a part of this total energy. Vast amounts of spiritual energy are waiting to be released.

Jesus knew how to release spiritual energy to a phenomenal degree. He healed all kinds of sickness by direct spiritual means, and He told us that we could do even greater works than His if we learned to channel this spiritual energy as He did.

When He told us to pray, "Deliver us from evil," Jesus faced the fact of destructive forces in nature as well as the fact of destructive forces in human nature. The last great phrase of the Lord's Prayer is the glorious affirmation that God holds the key to the conquest of evil. Jesus did not give us this phrase—the early Church added it: "For thine is the kingdom, and the power, and the glory for ever and ever." The early Christians could make this affirmation out of vivid experience. They had faith in God's power because they saw it at work to deliver them in spite of persecution, torture, martyrdom, sickness, death—the very worst life could do to them.

At its best, that has always been the faith of the church. Therefore, the application of direct spiritual power to sick bodies and minds—indeed to a sick world—is not only scientifically sound, but actually essential.

Again to quote Dr. Peale: "We are learning that faith properly understood and applied is a powerful factor in overcoming disease and establishing health."[14]

Many people have rejected the idea of spiritual healing as crackpot, indulged in by the lunatic fringe, and therefore not to be dabbled in by conventional and regular churchgoers. In the past few years, however, outstanding bishops and clergy in our various communions have come to believe differently. Prayers for healing as well as sacramental services for healing are now once more held regularly in our most orthodox churches. The laying on of hands and anointing with holy oil is again made use of as a means of healing grace.

In the early days of the Church, when little was known about medicine, surgery, drugs, and psychiatry, there were special and very beautiful prayers and services for the healing of the sick of body and mind. The Anglican Prayer Book contains many such prayers. On page 308 are special prayers for the sick. On page 320 there are prayers to be said in connection with anointing and the laying on of hands. On page 321, is a short service of Holy Communion for the sick.

Those of us who believe in direct spiritual healing feel that our doctors and scientists have been privileged to discover many effective material and psychological ways in which to heal body and mind. We are grateful for all these advances in material medicine, and gladly make use of them. Through the years deeply dedicated and unselfish men and women in medicine have done much to promote bodily health and long life. We feel, however, that the discovery of so many material ways to heal disease does not afford any good reason to discard the direct spiritual healing of disease. Material means of healing and spiritual means of healing should go hand in hand. Both are scientific.

A very fine, conscientious woman said to me, "I'm afraid of spiritual healing. I have a relative who is crippled; if I assured her that she could be healed through prayer and she wasn't, I would have raised her hopes and then dashed them. She would never believe in me or prayer again. I prefer to trust to the doctors; they are doing all that science can do and they do not raise any false hopes." People like this need the assurance that we who believe in spiritual healing do not wish to repudiate doctors and psychiatrists. We are grateful and wish to work with them. We believe God guides their efforts, as He guides ours through prayer.

Recently I had the privilege of talking with Dr. Alfred Price, rector of St. Stephen's Episcopal Church, Philadelphia. Dr. Price is a great believer in the Sacrament as the supreme means of healing. He is also a great believer in the power of united prayer in support of this Sacrament. In a letter he says:

We now have seventy-two hand-picked persons in our Prayer Fellowship. They join in a daily chain of prayers from 6 A.M. to midnight every day of the week. Some give fifteen minutes, while others give a half hour to an hour. We remember each needy person eighteen hours a day for a period of four weeks. Each person in the fellowship is disciplined to give a certain time each day. We have every hour covered over three times. We have business men whose secretaries disconnect the phone in the mid-afternoon while the boss takes out his devotional material and lifts up the sick and needy persons on the list for God's love and healing to go and surround them. Last year over fifteen hundred persons were prayed for. Each prayer partner receives a weekly list of some forty or fifty names with a thumbnail sketch of their needs.

The healings that have come about as the result of the prayers of Dr. Price and his group have been carefully documented. In his prayer group are doctors, nurses, and psychiatrists, as well as business men and housewives.

Many other men and women in our churches have been endowed with the gift of healing. Neither the Church nor modern medicine can any longer deny its validity. The Church of England has a great healing center, Milton Abbey, officially recognized by the Archbishop of Canterbury, which is dedicated to this purpose.

A person is divided into three parts, spiritual, mental, and physical. We can fall sick in any one of these three parts of us.

There is a spiritual despair known as the dark night of the soul. There is mental darkness and depression and confusion, and there is bodily illness. Any one of these can be induced and aggravated by disturbance in either or both of the other areas of our being.

The Gospel of St. John opens with these words: "The light shines in darkness, and the darkness has not overcome it" (John 1:5, R.S.V.). Archbishop Temple likens Jesus to a lighthouse throwing a great beam of light across a path of dark water. Any ship that comes into that beam of light does not go on the rocks, but is brought safely into the harbor. The promise is that we may bring those we love, those in sickness, those in despair and confusion of mind, into the beam of His light, so that in it they may find healing and peace and Easter victory.

All of us have experienced acute sorrow, tension, or frustration in our lives. Many of us have experienced severe physical suffering. There are times when we feel that it all adds up to darkness. That is why those words in St. John's Gospel are so comforting: "The light shines in the darkness, and the darkness has not overcome it." Let us try to keep this promise in mind as we attempt healing through prayer. We can pray this shining hope into people's bodies and minds and souls. It is one of our most glorious privileges as Christians to do so. We can learn to pray, singly and together, with the kind of hope Jesus had, with the kind of faith Jesus had. I believe we are intended to pray like that, I believe we are intended to see God's living power lighten darkened lives. If we have not had that experience we have not lived. It can happen to any single one of us, not just to people like Norman Vincent Peale. We may not be unusually gifted, but all of us can pray with faith, for the gift of prayer is offered to us all.

Illness of body is very concrete. It fills us with fear and pain. God stands ready to free us from fear and release us from pain. Two radiant friends of ours called long-distance from Toronto recently to say that they had just been privileged to be a part of a group that had been used to heal a man of leukemia. Think of that! These men are not crackpots. One of them is a well-known clergyman. One of them is a prominent business man. And they had actually seen this marvelous thing take place and be checked by the doctors.

I had a rich experience last autumn in connection with the healing of a child when I was visiting some dear friends in another city. These people were great believers in prayer. During my visit they told me of a young niece whose little boy had had a tragic accident the spring before.

One morning, while the mother was telephoning in an adjoining room, the two-year-old baby climbed up on the electric stove in the kitchen. The burners were all turned on and he had burned his feet and legs dreadfully before his mother had time to rescue him.

All that summer the doctors hoped that with the help of modern burn treatment his legs would heal by themselves. The young mother, during the hot weather, changed the bandages every day, but the legs did not heal.

Finally, in August the doctors suggested skin grafts as a last resort. At the end of two weeks the bandages were removed but the grafts had not taken. As the young mother has said to me since, "When I looked at his poor little legs and saw the great blisters where the grafts should have taken, and realized that the doctors had done all they could and that he might never walk again, I felt near to madness. I didn't think I could stand it. I didn't believe much in prayer, I didn't believe much in anything, but I knew Aunt Grace and Uncle John did, so I called them to pray very specially." (It was during my visit that the young mother, called.) "Aunt Grace's reply over the telephone was to say quietly, 'I have been praying for you, but there is someone visiting me who believes greatly in prayer. Tonight at ten o'clock we will pray together for you and the doctors and the baby. Will you please join us? We will lift up your baby into God's light and we will ask that the skin grafts will take.'"

So that night we met, the aunt and uncle, my daughter, who was with me, her fiancé, and myself. There we truly experienced Jesus' promise, "If two of you shall agree on earth as touching anything that they shall ask, it shall be done for them of my Father which is in heaven. For where two or three are gathered together in my name, there am I in the midst of them." Our unity of spirit that evening was like an electric current. We were given the deep assurance that all was well. Before I returned home, Aunt Grace told me the baby was recovering.

Two weeks later I received a letter from a strange young woman. I had never thought to ask Grace her niece's name. I knew only that she and her husband were two attractive, gay young marrieds who lived in a near-by suburb. Life was busy and good to them, and they did not bother with church or prayer or religion until this accident to their little boy. As I studied the envelope, I recognized the postmark as that of the suburb in which Grace's niece lived. The note inside was very moving. It read:

I don't know how to thank you and Aunt Grace for what you did after I asked for the prayers. The skin grafts took and the baby is going to be all right, and, what is more, I completely lost that awful feeling of despair, and knew that everything would work out. My husband and I hadn't thought much about religion before, but I want to promise you, Mrs. Shoemaker, from now on we are going to be steady and devoted members of the church.

She and her husband have made good their promise and have not only gone to church but have become one of the leading young couples in that church.

In this case the need of the young couple linked to our united prayer of faith released God's healing power into the body of the child as well as into the minds of the desperate parents.

I have often been asked, "What about the times when we pray for healing and the person is not healed? Is there something wrong with our faith when this happens? Or perhaps we are fooling ourselves and prayer is only some form of autosuggestion, which sometimes works and sometimes does not."

There are many reasons why prayers for healing seem at times not to be answered. One is that though we pray, our fear and anguish are stronger than our faith and we block God's power. The kind of prayer that is qualified by this reasoning is not much of a prayer. "Oh, God, if you can heal, please do," or, "I'm afraid this is too much even for you, but please help my sick friend." Or maybe even though we do not articulate our doubts, all the while we are praying we feel such fear and despair that our faith flickers like a candle in a heavy draft, and if the person for whom we pray dies, our faith dies with him.

This is not prayer, this is merely the projection of fear and anxiety.

Prayer is confident faith that we can bring our sick friends before God. It is confident faith that He loves them—that

His will for them is that they may have life, the kind of life and light and joy and well-being that is in Him.

In the next chapter I shall tell several stories of how He gives that light and life and joy and well-being, along with complete healing of the body, as well as with partial healing of the body, and sometimes without healing the body at all.

We human beings are so willful that unless our prayers are answered in exactly the way we visualize them being answered we often fail to see the answer when it comes. The people of true prayer are those who can see the answer when it is given in God's way, not theirs.

CHAPTER 15

How Prayer Frees Us From Fear
and Despair

THE GREATEST TRIUMPH OF FAITH I HAVE EVER WITNESSED happened to a friend of my husband's and mine. This story is particularly rich because a cancer was arrested after God had first released my friend from fear. Mrs. R is the able secretary of an outstanding minister. She is a wonderful and dedicated woman. And for some mysterious reason—who knows why?—good and wonderful people sometimes are called to face the most severe tests.

Many years ago Mrs. R had a breast operation which was highly successful. Four years ago she went to the doctor for a biannual routine checkup. After taking X-rays and studying them, the doctor called her into his office and said, "Mrs. R, I hate to tell you this, but these X-ray slides show that you have cancer in both lungs and in the bones of your chest. Ordinarily, a person with this trouble lives about six months. I am confident we can make you comfortable, but I cannot give you any hope."

She managed to get back to her apartment, and the first thing she did was to kneel down by her bed and ask God what to do. It came to her very clearly that she must come East and seek another diagnosis from the doctor who had performed the first operation.

The doctor in New York was less blunt than the doctor in the West. He indicated the X-rays might show trouble from an old bronchial condition, but he was afraid they confirmed the cancer diagnosis. He assured her, however, that he would give her the very newest treatment used to check cancer.

She came to us to recover herself, to find her bearings again, to get ready for whatever the future held. Bishop Pardue says a wonderful thing to people facing death. "You are so fortunate to know ahead, because you have time to prepare yourselves for the wonders of the after-life. So many people are given no time to prepare themselves."

At that time I was meeting every week with a small prayer group. We were not a group that had been meeting very long. Most of us were young in the life of prayer. I shall never forget the morning Mrs. R joined us and, at the end of the meeting, requested us to remain a moment, as she wished to ask a favor. Then she told us what she was up against and asked for our prayers. There is great power in standing in a circle and holding hands when there is some terrifically intense and urgent need for prayer. We stood in a circle that morning and we lifted Mrs. R before God with all the power we could summon, asking that she would be freed from all fear, and that He would give her light and peace.

She stayed with us a few more days and we had further prayer together. Then she went to visit her son. From there she wrote that she slept sixteen hours a day for two weeks, after which she returned to work, completely free of fear and determined to keep going as long as she could. Her letters for the past two years tell the rest of the victorious story.

January 13, 1951

"You have received my wire telling you of the results of my latest X-ray and the fact that the lung cancer is positively arrested, and the X-ray is better than the others. The hormone injections will be continued, however, as that seems wise.

"As I left the doctor's office all I could think of was 'Great and Glorious Are the Works of the Lord.' And then followed the thought that I shall have a longer time in which to work for Him. There is so much to do, and so very many people hungry for a faith and an inner conviction.

"As I am writing I recognize the utter change in one's values, and the tremendous gain in inner strength when one has, with God's help, attained complete freedom from fear, as He helped me to do through His grace, and power and love expressed from all the prayers that were being said for my healing."

June, 1951

"Helen, dear Helen, how wonderful this change that God makes in our lives! With the dread word 'cancer' one is first humanly filled with shock and creeping fear, but one day—so quietly God enters in—there is a sudden realization that all fear is gone—God has 'taken over' and will carry on the rest of the way."

January, 1952

"I have offered my services at any time to the doctor in the event he should have a patient in partial shock following a realization that he or she has cancer. I know I will be able to restore morale and witness for our Lord at the same time.

"Now I have been asked to lead the adult Bible Class of one of our new missions. There are seventy-seven families, all of them have children, young parents who are educated and very articulate, full of a desire to learn. They asked the bishop if he could get me to lead them. . . . Through a feeling of inadequacy I would have refused the responsibility had I not gone through this recent experience, which has so increased my feeling of obligation to our Lord.

"I started last Sunday. There were twenty-nine adults in the class, eleven of whom were men, two of them doctors. Of course I knew God was with me, but I have such a human, lazy tendency to lean on someone else and listen to them and there I sat with twenty-nine people looking at me pleasantly expectant!

"Everything about my life since July, 1947, has been so amazing, thrilling and dramatic! If anyone thinks that trying to be a Christian and to grow spiritually is dull, they just don't know!

"The doctor checked me again yesterday and I'm well. Keep me in your prayers, please!"

October 6, 1952

"I now have a large group of young mothers in our All Saints Mission who are praying more and more, and whom I call by phone (calling two or three key women who then call the others) to immediately pray for someone who may be seriously ill, or undergoing an operation. Three weeks ago a grandmother from one of our parishes telephoned me in great distress (it was at the time that all but one of the city clergy were at General Convention), saying that she needed a clergyman so badly.

"Her seventeen-year-old grandson had the day before been taken to the hospital with polio. The boy is an acolyte in our church, weighs two hundred pounds and is six feet three inches tall. Her distress was greatly relieved when I told her of the prayer group which I would alert for prayers for John's recovery. For three days the boy was dying—he was cyanotic, under oxygen, and the doctors could not foretell the outcome.

"Two days later his fever had gone, he was under hot packs, and has been having his treatment in the tank baths for over a week now.

"The sister in this Roman Catholic hospital told the grandmother it was prayer alone that saved the boy. As a result, now there is a group of women in that parish (as the word has gone around) on whom I can call. And the best thing is that each one of those women is deepening her own spiritual life in the process. Our Lord has also been using me in cancer cases. Women who have recently been operated on have their families telephone to ask me to call. It is so wonderful to be needed and to be used."

In July, 1953, Mrs. R had what seemed to be a return of cancer symptoms. With the same joyous trust she submitted to further treatment and again the X-ray showed the disease to have been arrested, with a further deepening of her trust and gratitude. Not only this, but she is constantly in touch with other victims of cancer, sharing her faith and courage with them. In August, 1954, comes Mrs. R's most recent word:

"Some day science will find a sure cure for cancer, but certainly I can demonstrate that, a real faith which dissipates fear and raises the morale helps to hold cancer back. . . . The treatment is based entirely on the spot shown on the X-ray. The spot on the right lung remains encapsuled and arrested."

This glorious story reads like the New Testament. The victory, the power, the joy, the outreach into other lives that God has given to Mrs. R. First she was delivered from fear, then from all preoccupation with her disease, and, lastly, she has been filled with such radiant light that she is a channel of that light and life to others.

Despair is an illness of the mind that always yields to prayer. Many people lead lives of quiet desperation. Too many anxieties, too many family crises, too many successive sorrows, too many responsibilities, or a long, discouraging illness often crack an otherwise strong and positive spirit.

One of the most loving and powerful Christians I know broke down under just such a series of pressures some years ago. He went South to recuperate. Rest did not help him, recreation did not help him. The kindness and advice of friends and doctors failed to reach him. He found himself floundering helplessly in a black pit of despair.

One day he flung himself down on his bed utterly defeated and overwhelmed. He faced once more the basic cause of his despair—there was mental instability in his family. It came from his mother's side. His dear brother, who had been a stable and steady citizen his whole life, died in a mental institution; three of his cousins had committed suicide. What chance had he against such powerful odds?

The verdict of his whole family background was against him.

Then, like a tiny crack of light in a black room, crept the thought that some people in his church back home were praying for him. Suddenly the conviction blazed into his mind that God loved him, that Christ was that very moment interceding for him. Therefore defeat and despair were completely contrary to God's will for him. He lay quietly under the impact of this thought until it grew and grew, filling the room with light.

He got up from that bed a completely new man, and the sense of God's love has never left him. Twice in his life since then he has been miraculously healed through the prayers of his friends, joined to his own deep trust in God's love, once of a nearly fatal virus pneumonia, and more recently of an all but fatal coronary thrombosis.

I know no one who radiates God's love as this man does. He is permeated with it and he releases it into every life he touches. Hundreds of alcoholics, neurotics, and even the most hardened criminals owe their restoration to him.

Recently a schoolteacher put into my hands the following moving account in the form of a composition of how a sixteen-year-old boy overcame illness and despair; it describes the confident faith that came to him through the prayers of his family and his friends.

"Yea, though I walk through the valley of the shadow of death I will fear no evil, for thou art with me."

You know the above passage from the Twenty-third Psalm. That passage helped me through my darkest moments of polio.

It all started over Labor Day week-end two years ago. I had been practicing football, going swimming, and dancing to late hours. Over the holiday week-end my parents and I drove back to my grandmother's. I was very tired and played out from the long trip, plus the strenuous activities. Monday night to

Wednesday night I had had no rest or sleep. Pains kept creeping up and down my weary back. After a long drive home, I thought that I would get better. The pains continued! Finally, Saturday morning I was rushed to the hospital in an ambulance.

I remember that ambulance ride vividly. My mother told me, whatever I saw or heard, to have faith in God and to remember the Twenty-third Psalm.

I had been put on the critical list at Municipal Hospital. Through many weeks of pain, I fought my battle to conquer polio. Because I had been placed in isolation I had no visitors —hospital rules. A patient is allowed to see only his doctor or minister.

One person I will never forget is my minister, Rev. Robert Penrose. He prayed with both me and my parents. Most important, he brought news and relief to my parents who could not see me.

All types of people prayed for my recovery—not only people of my own creed, but also from different creeds. The boys and teachers at school prayed for me. Our colored maid gathered together a group of people from her church, and they held prayer meetings for me during this week. Catholic friends went to mass in my behalf, and Jewish boys gathered in the temple. After I spent three weeks in the hospital, the doctors sent me down to the Home for Crippled Children.

When I first went down to the home I weighed ninety pounds. Some doctors thought that I might never walk again; others thought I would never see school again. Through many months of faith and prayer and the will to go on, I worked on my recovery from the dreaded disease.

After three months of hard work, I began to sit up with a big, heavy steel brace on my back. Some doctors said that I would never be able to get rid of that brace. Three months later I stood on my feet for the first time since I had been stricken. It took four people to hold me straight. The doctors said I would have to wear leg braces.

Today I don't walk with braces on my legs, and two months ago I threw away my back brace. Slowly but surely I am regaining my strength and the use of my muscles. The doctors say my case is a miraculous recovery. People ask me why! I reply, "Eighty to ninety per cent of my recovery is due to faith and prayer."

There are several things that I have learned from my sickness. I learned that faith and prayer can conquer. Along with that I have learned how to pray. A person in prayer should ask and believe that what he asks will be answered. In other words, a person should believe in what he is praying for, not pray just for the sake of praying. A person must also understand that his prayer might not be answered in the way he wants it to be answered, but as God wills it. In praying one should always ask God, "If Thou willest." The most important thing about prayer is to know that Someone is with you at all times. Just speak and He will hear.

A woman of fifty, the wife of a minister, who for years had had perfect health, and was a superb complement to her husband in all his work, was taken ill with a virus infection of the middle ear. She was a deeply dedicated woman, perfectly disciplined and selfless. She believed in healing prayer and prayed with some of the best-known leaders in spiritual healing; still her body was not suddenly healed. Perhaps, like Mrs. R and the lad with polio, she has received a greater gift. A recent letter from her tells what has come to her in this trouble:

I could write a book about the last year and a half, and what I believe about gradual healing as perfectly possible, as well as the sudden kind. What I have already learned with ups and some downs of great discouragement and despair has been that in spite of an ear which rings incessantly, when I am close to Christ nothing can keep me from hearing His voice; in spite of the fact that I still can stand only for a few minutes with any comfort, I can stand up for Christ wherever I am, and with people He wants helped; in spite of eyes which still can be used only an hour to read or write—that is, at one time—I pray that my spiritual vision will continue to grow and keep pace with Christ's plan. All in all, I am grateful to be alive, grateful that I can do a little more than a year ago, grateful that so many doors are opened that might be closed. I don't know, and no doctor seems to either, whether I will be completely well or whether there is permanent injury to a nerve or something.

Last May I faced what I have as a permanent handicap—something that may never be changed. The acceptance of that brought great peace. The important thing above all else is whether I can live on top of this condition or get defeated by it, due to very frustrating limitations. I know that if I abide in Him as He tells us to, I not only can live above it, but will live above it.

One of the things that makes Good Friday the deepest and most wonderful day of the Christian year is that then Jesus Himself went down into the black pit of despair for us. When we face our own Good Fridays of fear and despair we remember, too, His final words: "Father, into thy hands I commend my spirit." His last word was a word of trust and love, and God vindicated His trust and love with the triumph of Easter morning.

Easter was not only an event in history. Easter is the triumph of faith over fear, despair and discouragement. It means the revival of our souls and the rebirth of hope and courage. The people whom I have just described have experienced this revival and this rebirth.

CHAPTER 16

How Prayer Helps Those In Sorrow

JESUS FACED THE FACT OF DEATH AS HE FACED THE FACT OF evil. If we are to pray compassionately and helpfully for those facing death or those in intense sorrow we need to understand better what our faith teaches us in regard to death and life.

Our prayers for the comfort of those in sorrow and those facing death often seem not to rise above the ceiling because we ourselves think of death as the ultimate enemy rather than the gateway to life. We think of it as separation from all the dear familiar places and associations and people which spell our earthly security. We think of it as walking out into the night, alone and naked, with no light to guide us. We think it writes *finis* to our dearest relationships. It is something we shrink from with utter dread.

This attitude towards death is totally unchristian. In

almost every word and act Jesus sought to dispel it. He said, "I came that ye might have life and have it more abundantly." On Easter He not only walked out of death into life, but out of apparent defeat into final victory. Here He demonstrated His greatest claim. "I am the resurrection and the life: he that believeth in me, though he were dead, yet shall he live, and whosoever that liveth and believeth in me shall never die." (John 11:25; 26).

It is this great fact He is asking us to believe and transmit to others. In other words, He is saying, "Trust me, trust my love for you. I am alive, I am praying for you. When the time comes for you to join me, I will call for you and you will come. At that time you will truly live, not subject to the aches and pains and problems and limitations of your life on earth, but free to exercise every gift of mind and personality I have given you. In this life there will be no bodily disease to hamper you, no selfishness, no pride or lust for power to block the growth of your personality, no limiting actions of other people to warp or frustrate the full development of all your gifts, no slavery to temptations of the flesh, no subtle poison of self-deception. Abide in me while you are on earth. I have shown you the way, so that when you come to me over here you will abide with me always."

As He has opened the gate of life to us, so He asks us to open it to others.

A wonderful old friend of mine, Mrs. M, was visiting in a hospital one day. As she entered the elevator a flurried looking nurse pushed a young man in on a stretcher and said tensely to the elevator boy, "Operating room, emergency, please."

The young man on the stretcher looked terrified and my old friend leaned over him and smiled at him tenderly. He grasped her hand and gasped: "Lady, do you pray?" She nodded. He held her hand very tight and closed his eyes, "I don't know any prayers," he mumbled, "and I'm so scared I might die."

So there in the ascending elevator Mrs. M prayed very simply that Christ would surround the boy with His love, take the boy's fear, and give him His peace. The elevator reached the operating floor, and the nurse wheeled him away with a grateful backward look at Mrs. M.

The following day Mrs. M was again at the hospital and as she walked down the corridor the nurse of the day before caught up with her and stopped her. She put her hand on Mrs. M's arm. "Thank you for what you did yesterday," she said simply.

"Oh, I'm so glad you sought me out," replied Mrs. M. "I came today hoping to find you and hear how our boy got on."

"He's all right," replied the nurse. "Before he went under the anesthetic he said, 'Tell the lady it's all right, I'm not afraid any more, because God is here.' That was the last thing he ever said, because he died on the operating table."

I have often asked myself whether I would have been as alert and ready to share my faith as Mrs. M was with that needy, dying boy. Often we are not aware of it, because too often we are preoccupied with ourselves and our own thoughts, but almost no day passes in which we do not have an opportunity to encourage or comfort or help someone. And not an hour passes when our prayers cannot open the gate of life to someone somewhere.

The following letter describes better than I can what prayer can do to uphold a person in deep sorrow. This woman came from a fine and intelligent agnostic family. Until trouble struck her she had no faith in a personal God or personal Saviour.

Her first husband died after a long illness, her second husband died suddenly two years ago, and her youngest son was killed in Korea. Through these ordeals she has found a depth and understanding and a greatness of soul that I believe few people find. My husband and I were with her at the time of her second husband's death, but were on the other side of the country when her son was killed.

We phoned her on the day the body of her son was brought home from Korea. He had been a brilliant young flyer, one of the heroes of World War II. Yet he was used again in Korea because they were so short of pilots out there. After the burial service she wrote as follows to us:

I was sustained all day by the Presence. And I know He was there. Perhaps I would have been fully conscious of the Spirit if I had not been thinking of your prayers and human understanding and longing to help, but I don't think so. It seems odd that in hours so terrible one goes into a world far beyond any human help or comfort, stark, staring, alone and suffering. When there is only one possible strength to turn to, you are forced to turn to Him, for there is nothing else.

If I were what I would call a convinced atheist, I am sure I would have to do that. And to me it is the final proof there is a God. You simply are forced to turn to Him, and I am sure that there has never been a soul in the finality of his own death, or that of those who are closer to him than himself, husband or child, that has not done so.

But what I meant when I started saying, "It seems odd," is, it is when you are alone there with only God you then become suddenly conscious of others, of human beings, friends, as I did at the grave, and at the very last seem to feel around you all the prayers of your friends over the past months. What an extraordinary sensation!

It was true that a number of us had held her steadily in prayer for months, and during this time we almost threw a cordon of prayer around her.

Two other dear friends lost their only daughter in a fearful motor accident this past Thanksgiving. In a beautiful appreciation of their daughter, the father tells of the way in which God has interpreted to them their daughter's going.

Nancy's witness for Christ always amazed me. It continued wherever she went, although at the same time she entered into all good times and was so often "the life of the party."

In high school she became an outstanding leader, and at college last autumn was elected president of her freshman dormitory, and through it all she influenced so many for good.

Just as I write this a letter comes from a college friend saying, "Whenever I had a problem I'd go to Nancy. She'd listen to my petty troubles with interest and we'd hash it out, and before I knew it I would forget them and everything would be fine. She was always so understanding."

Our daughter is not dead. She lives. I know she is closer to me now than ever before. She walks with me and talks with me, and it is a wonderful joy to have her with me always.

When I conduct a burial now, I find myself saying silently, especially if I know the person hasn't been a very good practicing Christian: "Nancy, someone else is coming over who needs help!"

Furthermore, Nancy lives on in the lives of her high-school classmates, who started a memorial fund for her in the high school. And she will live on in the lives of the students who shall come after her, for each year a member of the graduating class who is chosen as the student "who has shown the most concern, interest, and love for fellow students during the high-school years" will receive a special scholarship award in her memory. . . .

She is living on, too, in reconciled lives—lives restored and uplifted because of her life, and especially because of her death. For instance, there is the high-school boy who was always somewhat dejected and retiring, whose changed expression gives evidence to the truth of what he said to me the day after the burial service, "Something has happened to me; I'm different. Nancy's death has made me think for the first time in my life. I know what she believed and I believe it now too!"

She lives on, especially in our family, as we continue to serve God. Nancy had been asked to sing at the wedding of one of her best schoolmates. Her mother sang in her place, although it was only two weeks after the burial. And her mother continues to play the organ, direct the choir, and live into the lives of piano pupils. It hasn't been easy; there have been many tears, but I know there is an inner peace that passes understanding.

Yes, she sparkled with joy all her life, and I believe she will continue to sparkle as she goes on to perfection. If there is a band in heaven I am sure she will have it out to welcome us on that great day of reunion when God says our work in this life is finished.

On the headstone we shall soon erect on the beautiful spot overlooking the Hudson where she is buried will appear St. Paul's words to the Colossians: "Christ in you the hope of Glory."[15]

What these people have experienced is a grace not their own. They have known the soul strength that comes through the fact that in our darkest hours we are upheld by the love and prayers of those "who are for us" in both worlds. I say in both worlds, for I firmly believe that "those we have loved long since and lost awhile" are constantly watching over us from the other world. They know our fear and pain and human despair. They know, because they too experienced these things in their earthly life. Now, freed from these limitations, they join their prayers to the human prayers of those who love us here, so that together we may walk forward into the life to which Jesus blazed the trail.

PART III

Again I say unto you, That if two of you shall agree on earth as touching any thing that they shall ask, it shall be done for them of my Father which is in heaven. For where two or three are gathered together in my name, there am I in the midst of them.

MATTHEW 18:19; 20.

CHAPTER 17

The Power of United Prayer

IT HAPPENED IN THE PARISH HALL OF CALVARY CHURCH, NEW YORK, which had just been decorated with six or eight large posters of white elephants rampant in preparation for a white elephant sale the following day. Tonight it was packed to the doors with three hundred people at a "Faith That Works" meeting, at which laymen spoke of their experience of faith at work in their daily lives.

As I prepared to come downstairs (we lived on the top floor of our parish house), the telephone rang. I answered rather impatiently, for I was late. It was Anna, one of our young adult leaders. She was very much upset.

Alice, her roommate, had just been rushed to a large city hospital, desperately ill with internal hemorrhages. The doctors were giving her transfusions, but were not sure they could save her. I asked how it had happened. Anna didn't know. She had come home from work in answer to a phone call from Alice and found her alone and apparently bleeding to death. She said Alice hadn't seemed well that morning and when they separated for work, Anna had suggested that she come home early.

I reassured Anna, told her one of the clergy would join her at the hospital immediately, and rushed downstairs. All the way down in the elevator I kept saying, "God, what shall I do, how can I help?"

Suddenly it came to me. Alice was the girl who had painted all the white elephants which were dancing so gaily around the walls of our parish hall. I would ask the group in the hall to pray with me for her healing.

Fortunately, I found our young assistant minister in the front hall as I stepped out of the elevator. I told him what the situation was, what I planned to do, and dispatched him to the hospital.

I squeezed into the back of the hall and sent a note up to my husband, who was leading the meeting, and he called me to the platform. As I mounted, I pointed to the white elephants cavorting on all sides of us and said, "Do you like these white elephants?"

The crowd nodded and smiled. I told them why they were there and continued, "The girl who came down here and spent her day off doing them for me is lying at death's door in the operating room of one of our city hospitals this minute. She is an orphan, just one of the pretty, talented girls who make a living in this city. There is no one to pray for her except us and a few friends. Will you pray with me for her?"

We bowed our heads—all three hundred of us. I cannot remember what I said, but I felt as I said it as though three hundred pairs of hands lifted that lonely child with me, and held her steadily and unitedly before God. Then there was a moment of deep, united silence. The meeting went on. I returned upstairs to await another phone call from Anna. One half hour later it came. All was well, Alice had turned the corner and would live.

A few days later I visited Alice in the hospital. She was very pale and pretty as she lay in bed, her big hazel eyes bigger than ever, and her black hair a lovely frame around her small, heart-shaped face.

She took my hand and said, "Oh, Mrs. Shoemaker, how I have wanted to see you and tell you how much you and all those people have done for me. I thought I was going to die and felt so alone, and here I am surrounded by friends. Will you thank them for me? I have been coming to church, but I didn't understand it very well. I think I came to please Anna, but now I know that God is real and that He loves me and that He healed me, and I want to say, 'Thank you,' for the rest of my life."

Alice not only got well, but was married shortly after. The "Faith That Works" group contributed their quarters and dollar bills for a beautiful Bible, which we sent her as a wedding present and reminder of that night of united prayer, when we had all been privileged to share in her healing.

How well I remember some of the people who crowded around me to give their quarter or dollar bill for that Bible —two poor little Negro women, a physiotherapist, an old man who lived alone in a hotel room, a young couple, several office workers, the switchboard operator, a public-school teacher. These people all felt as though Alice belonged to them in a special sense, and they wanted to show their love.

Some time after this a very dearly loved relative of Alice's was taken ill. Remembering her own experience, Alice wired us, and alerted the minister and people of the church she had gone to as a child. A very large group came together for prayer, and Alice feels that her young relative's life was saved because of it. Alice believes in the power of united prayer, because she has tested it in the test tube of personal experience.

There has grown up among many Christians the false idea that when we pray we must pray alone and in private. True, Jesus said: "When thou prayest, enter into thy closet, and when thou hast shut thy door, pray to thy Father which is in secret; and thy Father which seeth in secret himself shall reward thee openly (Matthew 6:6). But we have taken this verse out of its context. Here Jesus is inveighing against the show-off, the Pharisee who wanted everyone to know he was a good, prayerful man and took every opportunity to parade his piety in public. In contrast to this is the publican whose prayers are sincere and humble and selfless.

Jesus is not talking against united prayer here, He is talking against fake piety and insincerity and exhibitionism. If He did not believe in united prayer He would not have urged it on His followers as strongly as He does in the following passage: "Again I say unto you, That if two of you shall agree on earth as touching anything that they shall ask, it shall be done for them of my Father which is in heaven. For where two or three are gathered together in my name, there am I in the midst of them."

In his superb little booklet, *The Secret of Intercession,* Dr. Andrew Murray reminds us of the vital importance of united intercession with these words:

God's intense longing to bless seems in some sense to be graciously limited by His dependence on the intercession that rises from the earth. . . . God regards intercession as the highest expression of His people's readiness to receive and to yield themselves wholly to the working of His almighty power. Christians need to realize this as their true nobility and their only power with God—the right to claim and expect that God will hear prayer. God rules the world and His Church through the prayers of His people. That God should have made the extension of His kingdom to such a large extent dependent on the faithfulness of His people in prayer is a stupendous mystery and yet an absolute certainty.

Jesus started the first prayer group on the night of the Last Supper, when, after an immortal hour of teaching and preparation, He led His disciples in the greatest prayer ever prayed, the High Priestly Prayer of St. John 17.

In this prayer Jesus emphasizes again and again His oneness with His Father, His disciples' oneness with Him, and His and His Father's and His followers' oneness with us. He weaves us all into one united, unbreakable strand.

We can imagine His meetings with His people for prayer and encouragement and fellowship after His resurrection. Then in the Book of Acts we have the record that, in obedience to His command, "these all continued with one accord in prayer and supplication, with the women, and Mary the mother of Jesus, and with his brethren" (Acts 1:4).

Further on we have account after account of the apostles and their converts meeting in secret upper rooms for prayer.

The Service of Morning Prayer in the Anglican Book of Common Prayer closes with the words of St. Chrysostom, Bishop of Constantinople in 398 A.D.

Almighty God, who hast given us grace at this time with one accord to make our common supplications unto thee; and dost promise that when two or three are gathered together in thy Name thou wilt grant their requests; Fulfil now, O Lord, the desires and petitions of thy servants, as may be most expedient for them; granting us in this world knowledge of thy truth, and in the world to come life everlasting. Amen.

Notice the word "common" and the word "servants." "Common" here means united, and "servants" means us, not me alone.

St. Chrysostom and the writers of the Prayer Book understood very well that the Church was a family, a group of people bound together by a common loyalty to a common Father. They wanted to make sure that no future generations would forget this, so they concluded the service of morning worship with this beautiful corporate intercession.

So group prayer is in the great tradition of the Christian Church, instituted by our Lord Himself and carried on by His disciples. The written prayers of the New Testament and the Prayer Book are the crystallization of the free and passionate prayers coming spontaneously from full hearts to the lips of these followers of Christ.

CHAPTER 18

The Value of Family Prayer

THERE ARE VARIOUS WAYS IN WHICH WE CAN PRAY UNITEDLY. THE first way is in the family. The family is the God-ordained group. Most of us have a family, and it is intended, according to the Divine plan, that God should be the central figure of our family life.

Every morning all over the United States millions of doors are opened—black doors, green doors, red doors, white doors, shabby doors, neat doors—and every morning millions of men and women and children stream out through these doors to school, to work, to market. What is in the hearts of all the people from all these homes whose doors open into the world? Is there uneasiness, resentment, fear about the future? Or is there confidence, faith, joy and hope, the hallmarks of a Christian people?

If we were to buttonhole these folk as they hurry past us, I fear the majority of answers would express the first state of mind, and part of the blame would be laid at the feet of Mr. Malenkov, and of the struggling world leaders who, so far, have failed to guide the feet of the world into the ways of peace.

Whatever the cause, this lack of unity, faith, and joy in living reflects itself in the average American family—or perhaps the average American family's lack of these qualities reflects itself in the inharmonious and uneasy state of society at large. We cannot expect a healthy society when, in one year alone, 500,000 divorces were granted in our courts, with the resultant dislocation of children's lives and emotions. As if this were not bad enough, alongside of the broken homes are millions of pagan homes in which a generation of children are being brought up spiritually illiterate, with no understanding of the great moral and spiritual laws that govern all life and therefore no knowledge of how to co-operate with them. Recently our newspapers have been publishing a series of articles on vandalism in our public schools. This is one inevitable result of the moral and spiritual breakdown in the American home.

What is the solution? For every problem has a solution. Does it lie in the restoration of a faith that will dignify our existence and give us a cause worth living for? And has the family a part to play in the restoration of this faith?

There is a popular radio program entitled, "The Family That Prays Together Stays Together." A family is like a small orchestra. It needs a conductor who will see that each instrument is kept tuned and played in harmony with every other instrument. Then that family will make harmonious sounds within the walls of its own home that will carry out through the doors to the community at large.

The old idea of parental authority seems to be outmoded, but there must be some authority, some final point of reference, or there is no unity. Who, then, is good enough, consistent enough, authoritative enough, to conduct our family orchestra? Who indeed but God Himself? Therefore it is inescapable logic that we should turn back to family prayers and give the Divine Conductor an opportunity to tune us up and draw us together.

Just because some of us carry unpleasant memories of family prayers is no excuse to abandon them altogether. The present lack of any common family discipline or devotion is no adequate substitute for former unrealities. We need to try again. There never has been anything wrong with family prayers, while there may have been much wrong with those conducting them. Let us resolve to be real and humble and believing ourselves, and then family prayers cannot help but succeed.

A real obstacle to family prayer is the bedlam the average American family faces in the early mornings. There is the task of getting the household up, breakfast cooked, the coffee made, Peggy and Tom, Jr., ready for school, Tom, Sr., off to work, which altogether is no mean accomplishment, especially if it is to be managed in good order and in good temper.

Let us take a typical American family—Tom and Margaret Allen, who live in one of those small, trim new homes, in a vast new housing development on the edge of a large city. Tom and Margaret have decided to experiment with my proposal. So they get up fifteen minutes earlier than usual and ask Peggy and Tom, Jr., and Tom's mother, who lives with them, to do the same.

For once, the whole family arrives at the breakfast table simultaneously instead of in relays. Tom picks up the Bible, which has been dusted for the occasion, and reads a passage, after which he proposes a short time of silent prayer so that the passage read may make its particular appeal to each listener. It is surprising how much new truth is continually revealing itself to us in long familiar Bible passages.

Then Tom reads a prayer from that matchless little booklet, *Prayers New and Old,* or the Book of Common Prayer, or any other manual of prayers, which contains prayers for every mood and every occasion. This draws the family together so that they feel free to ask for prayers for some particular problem or person most on their hearts.

Peggy is worried about her school work. Young Tom has a big football game coming up. Tom, Sr., is contemplating a new business venture. Tom's mother has some sick friends. The whole family is concerned about the United Nations and Russia and China, and what the United States should do about the problems they represent.

These prayers are very brief and at the end all join in the Lord's Prayer, or the Apostles' Creed or St. Francis's great prayer. It does not take more than fifteen minutes, but each member of the family goes through the front door that morning feeling somehow warmed, close to one another, in tune with God, steadied and strengthened, and all deciding in their hearts that they will try to do it every day.

It is one thing to decide something. Who is to carry out the decision? Why, Tom, of course, as the head of the house. So I will give you a few suggestions, Tom, on how to keep the family prayer time fresh and vital.

There are certain things you must keep in mind—worship, praise, intercession, listening, affirmation. Let me emphasize, too, that a few moments of united silence should be a part of every morning prayer time so that the Great Conductor may give to each of us His solution to, or His guidance for, our particular concern. One important warning —don't allow yourselves to become skeptical about what one small unit like yourselves can accomplish.

Remember, you are one of thousands of similar units spread like a great net across the world. It will thrill your children to realize that they are part of this world family— part of the basic structure of a sound world society. Each little family unit like yours becomes a member of the world family as the prayers of each reach out and fuse with the Great Conductor's creative plan for His world. The Perfect Society is in His mind, it remains for us, His instruments, to play the harmonies that will translate it into actuality—and where better to start than in communion with Him around our breakfast tables?

There are three positive results of family prayer that I would like to stress. The first is that every member of a family who consciously and continually turns to "Our Father" for inspiration will find that he or she begins to see the others with new eyes. Where formerly we were critical and resentful of each other's faults, and often blind to our own, we begin to come to a new self-knowledge and a new patience.

We become less aware of the other fellow's sins, and more aware of what we may be doing to contribute to them. In other words, we begin to look at our brother or sister or father or mother-in-law or husband or wife with creative and understanding eyes rather than with critical and resentful eyes. It dawns upon us that if we pray in faith for a different member, little by little a new element comes into the situation, a new hopefulness in us, and in them a new openness of heart toward us and toward God.

The habit of family prayer can create an atmosphere in which problems of growing children are worked out both more intelligently and with less strain on all concerned than usually is the case. Following is the account of the solution of the schoolwork problem of a fifth-grade child, sent to me by a mother who has always included family prayers as part of the family's day.

Jane was a straight "A" pupil for the first three years. In the fourth grade she started to slip, and in the fifth grade she received "A" in music and health only.

My human reaction was one of disgust, but when I prayed about it, this is the thought that came: "You often lose your way in trying to do your best, and need help from other people in order to find it again. Jane has lost her way. She does not know how to use her mind. Ask her to write out for you the ways you can help her." This is what she wrote out.

"1. Make me study every afternoon at 5 o'clock.

"2. Tell me what books to bring home.

"3. Ask me to read a paragraph and then tell you what I have read."

For six weeks her father worked with her. At first the sessions were long and stormy. After three weeks, one-half hour sufficed. After five weeks her card showed marked improvement, and soon after Jane was able to study alone at 5 o'clock. Now, because her work is accurate, she seldom has home work, and her card satisfies parents and teachers.

The praying mother and father turned to God for help with their child; then they made a personal sacrifice to carry out the direction that God gave them, and the problem was solved.

The second positive result of family prayer is a sense of common purpose. We come to realize that we have been placed in our family for a reason. To put it very simply, God has a plan for us as a family. What higher adventure can we imagine than finding the part we are to play in carrying out that plan?

Third, family prayer develops in us a sense of world citizenship. We learn to live together creatively, we learn to act as a team to meet human need, and we learn to concern ourselves with God's world. Family prayer is the best cure I know for the insular point of view, for racial or national prejudice. The need of the world becomes our concern. Little children have a natural sense of world citizenship, as illustrated by this prayer of a five-year-old child.

Dear Jesus, please be with all the little children who are hungry, especially the Germans, the Koreans, and the Africans, and please make your peace all over them and all over the world.

In one fine American family of my acquaintance the hour for family worship is at the end of dinner in the evening. That seems to be the time when the family is most likely to be assembled.

The father always reads a Psalm, then the whole family get down on their knees around the dining table, while the father prays first for absent members, and then leads in the Lord's Prayer or one of our other universal prayers.

This quarter hour of united worship has been observed since the children were old enough to attend. Most of them are grown and married now, and their babies have joined the circle. No one is asked whether he would care to attend—all are automatically included, guests, new in-laws, anyone who happens to be present.

One of the grown sons tells the story of the time, during World War II, when the oldest boy, who was in the Navy, had been alerted for Okinawa and was sailing at midnight. Another son was at Camp Lejeune, a daughter at college, the youngest son at prep school, and a little sister at home.

The father arranged a telephone hookup at the usual dinner time, and promptly on the dot, with the whole family listening in, he carried them all through the customary service of family worship, including them all in his blessing, especially commending the boy going into battle.

It was a time none of them will ever forget—the familiar voice, the familiar words, the sense of family solidarity, and, above all, their common faith in God's all-embracing love and care.

If we can get across to our children that sense of the concern of God with the affairs of the whole world, that sense of being channels of His power, I believe that they are not likely to lose it as they go through life. We need not worry about the results of such a family adventure. God Himself will take care of the results. We need worry only about our share in the total effort, so that the influence of our family prayers, combined with that of others, may carry far and wide.

God is standing outside the doors of our homes—the black doors, the green doors, the red doors, the white doors, the shabby doors, and the neat doors. Shall we open those doors to Him and invite Him into our family circle? He is waiting for us to do just that.[16]

CHAPTER 19

Prayer Groups in the Church

How can the power of united prayer affect a church, and through a church influence a whole community?

The fellowship of the church will not be renewed by you as an individual. You cannot go to the people and say, "This church ought to be friendlier and warmer." That is the direct approach, which does not recognize that fellowship comes indirectly. What we must do is to form a small, natural group within the parish. This group must share deeply worship, Bible reading, study, and missionary interest. You must share with one another on the deepest level, even though it will seem awkward at first, your faith, your questions, your doubts, your dreams. Such a group will do more than many sermons to wake a sleeping congregation, and deepen our own lives. The same thing, of course, can be achieved in clusters at conferences, but for the real revival of the parish they should exist at the local level.

One of the things which often bothers me is how little we

really know each other. Each one of us is like a fortress, with
his ego bottled up inside. The shy woman hides in her fortress,
and never lets you see her. The cynical man throws up the shield
of his cynicism so you may not see him. And how often all the
gay talk and business are walls behind which we hide our true
belief and honest doubts! How seldom we really meet another
person or share deeply the things that would make us friends!
How often in business sessions and efficient organizations we
miss the one thing for which our hearts long and the Lord wants
of us! And because we do not really share, our work is thin
and we are still hungry! I read some time ago of the conferences
which Dwight L. Moody held for young men interested in the
Church's work. They met sometimes for three weeks for prayer
and study and fellowship; and from those conferences, with real
zeal, men went to the ends of the earth. I want you to form such
a group. Share the Bible in the method mentioned previously!
Share prayer! Share yourselves! In a small group, forgetting about
numbers, let the Lord reveal how deeply united souls can be in
Him.[17]

In Calvary Church, Pittsburgh, the church of which my
husband is now the rector, fifteen prayer study groups have
sprung up, one or two of which meet every day of the week.

There is a group of young married women who meet
every Friday morning for study and intercession; their young
husbands meet every Wednesday at a downtown club for
luncheon; a third group of women over sixty hold special
intercessions for the sick before a mid-week healing service.
Two groups of business women meet at the cathedral on
Tuesdays and Thursdays, stealing a half hour every week
from their precious luncheon recess. Five groups of middle-
aged housewives meet for study and prayer in each other's
homes; a young couples group meets Wednesday nights, and a
middle-aged couples group meets Thursday evenings, and so on.

Some of these groups emerged out of a six-week school

of prayer which I conducted in our parish during this past winter, others out of a course on basic Christianity taught by my husband. Besides these, two morning prayer programs have been started in the Homestead Plant of the United States Steel Company by an instrument man who is one of our parishioners. Of these Homestead programs I shall say more in the next chapter.

Each of these groups has chosen different books of the New Testament for study, rotates its leadership every week, and chooses its own prayer concerns. There are certain united intentions, however, which bind us all together.

At 7:30 each morning all of us pray unitedly for world peace, for our President, for the conversion of Russia, and for our clergy, and for our church. We have also prayed together for a sick teen-age child in our parish. This child had a rare disease, for which as yet medical science has not discovered the cure. The disease induced a spastic condition which affected her speech and the control of her hands and feet. As she became increasingly ill we all agreed that we would pray daily that "God would supply all her needs and that she might be encouraged and strengthened."

The hope that this united support brought to her and her family was wonderful to watch. They all have felt help pouring in hourly. It has been a joy to visit that home. The shining, selfless love of the parents and the shining beauty of that child's soul in a weak and helpless body have been truly inspiring. You can imagine the effect on all of these new young prayer groups, of this child's radiant courage. She herself wrote a beautiful prayer which she sent to each of us:

Almighty God, my lord, who has brought me safely through the trial of my life and has been my friend, companion and guiding light, I thank Thee for the friends who have been channels of Thy faith, love and courage. I thank Thee for the miracles of Christ which were revealed to me by the ministry of the Church. I pray that I may remember the debt I owe to God and pay it in service to others like me.

Since this page was written, this radiant child has gone to meet her "friend, companion and guiding light." If "Life is the anteroom for the great interview with the King," then surely she is standing before Him now.

Soon after their groups had begun, the young couples were put to a real test. The baby son of one of them fell desperately ill with dysentery. Immediately a member of the group telephoned all the others and a prayer chain of special intention was formed. We prayed around the clock for that little one and his parents.

> Prayer is an appeal to the friendship of God. . . . If we are God's friends, and come as such to Him, we must prove ourselves the friends of the needy; God's friendship to us and ours to others go hand in hand. When we come thus we may use the utmost liberty in claiming an answer.[18]

These young people, many of them new to the idea of united intercessory prayer, gave their whole hearts to their intention. The parents of the baby said afterwards that they could feel courage and poise and trust flowing into them, and the baby, who had been so ill that my husband had gone to the hospital for an emergency baptism late at night, suddenly and unpredictably began to get better.

Later the doctor so often jokingly referred to the fat, healthy, pink-cheeked cherub that he became as his "miracle baby." That was a year and a half ago. The young married prayer groups have grown and deepened since then; each member, besides meeting regularly for united prayer, is taking outstanding responsibility in the church; some teach in the church school, some are officers in the Men's Club, one has been elected to the vestry, and all are on call to help with any emergency that may arise.

In September we held a prayer group reunion. There are some two hundred persons in these various groups. What spiritual dynamite for a parish! One person spoke for each group, and you may like to read briefly what these people have been experiencing.

The first speaker was a middle-aged woman whose son had fought in the front lines in Korea. Her group is most remarkable because six months ago the members were practically strangers to each other. These women were of different background, different tastes and different church affiliations, yet all have the same spirit.

Here we are [she said] twelve people who six months ago were practically strangers—seven from this church and five from others. A number of us had never even met before.

As the weeks have gone by we have, through fellowship and the medium of prayer, become very close. All masks are off. We are completely ourselves, sincerely and uncritically loving one another. This warmth and concern for each other has been a startling revelation to all of us. It's something that just miraculously happened. Why are we so surprised to find ourselves acting the way God expects us to?

We all realize that this same wonderful thing can happen to anyone. So, as a future goal, we are going to try to get this knowledge across to others. One of the girls said, "And to think of what we've been missing all these years!" Her particular resolve is to try to pass this on to her two children, of college age, and to young people generally.

One of our members finds this little group particularly precious because it's different from all the other things she belongs to. It isn't something we joined because it was the thing to do, or because of the people who belonged. We're all there because we want to be, because we're desperately aware of an emptiness in our lives.

That is how we feel. . . . Now, what have we done?

We have learned to enjoy the Bible as we never did before. You would think that we had been brought up as heathen who had never known the Bible. Somehow, everything just seems new and different.

Our meetings have gone along without a definite system of leaders. Someone is always ready and willing to take over. Most of all, we are learning to pray—at the meetings, at home, and when alone. We've found out, too, that praying isn't easy. It demands thought, and our minds are lazy.

Slowly we're becoming articulate, gaining confidence, losing that almost painful self-consciousness that we had, and I'm sure that here, if in no other place, we come close to true humility— so aware are we of our shortcomings.

The subjects of our prayers are changing too—more for others, less for ourselves. The emphasis has shifted to God and to larger things. We pray for peace, for our country, other nations, all leaders and all people, the United Nations and the Church Universal.

One little characteristic of our group is that those who are absent always pray with us, wherever they are, from 10:30 to 11:30 on Thursdays, and of course we pray for them.

During the last six months of my son's year in Korea, most of which time he was in the front lines, I found strength, courage, and actual tranquility, knowing that our little group was constantly praying for him. Thursday was always my best day.

Another spokesman, a young husband this time, told what the middle-aged couples group, which meets on Thursday nights, has been experiencing:

The fundamental purpose of our prayer group is to dedicate ourselves to prayer for others and the welfare of our Lord's Kingdom. We feel that the prayers of several can be more effective than those of just one alone. We felt from the start that it was necessary to understand the basic elements of prayer, and to endeavor to incorporate these into our prayers.

Our group consists of six couples who meet regularly every Thursday night. A different moderator is chosen for each meeting to lead the prayer and discussion periods. Our prayer session lasts for about thirty minutes and the discussion for forty-five minutes. During the prayer portion of our program the moderator uses the basic form of Evening Prayer from the Book of Common Prayer, including the prayer for all sorts and conditions of men, and supplements these prayers with others taken from any source. At one point in our service everyone participates by offering his own spontaneous prayer. Such prayers may vary from supplications for a particular person's health to prayers for world peace, the United Nations, our parish, etc.

For the discussion period we have read the four gospels, being particularly aware of reference to our Lord's own prayers and instructions which He gave us for praying.

The value of any such endeavor can be measured only by its accomplishments. We feel that we have learned at least some of the basic principles of prayer. We feel that we know better how to pray and how to express ourselves.

As we look back we now recognize that our prayers at the start were quite narrow in scope. Today they are not only supplications, but they express thanks and praise to God.

We feel that the Christian fellowship of our group has helped us all. The fact that we know we will be understood by everyone is quite reassuring. We find that we are more willing to talk about God and prayer to others among whom we would not have mentioned the subject previously. Since ours is a couples group, many discussions of the subject have developed at home— a good influence on each of us individually, and on our entire families.

We believe we have become more objective in our outlook on life in general and more sympathetic to the views and opinions of others. Most important of all is a greater recognition of God's presence at all times, and a greater appreciation of the power of prayer.

These are only two reports of the twelve who reported that memorable evening. The others were equally individual and powerful. A parish is indeed blessed when it is permeated with such prayer power.

The members of these groups have not only grown in an understanding of the power of prayer in their own lives and in the life of the church, but they are being used to help other individuals and other groups to discover this same power. The couples groups visited a Methodist church one evening and helped to start a couples group there. Women from the different women's groups have visited other churches and women's clubs and established groups where they have visited.

Again to quote Andrew Murray: "Who can say what power a church can develop and experience if it gave itself to the work of prayer day and night for the coming of the kingdom?"[19]

If every church, not just a few churches in this great country of ours, were releasing creative spiritual energy into the bloodstream of our country through the kind of prayer Mr. Andrew Murray describes, who can foretell what kind of hope and leadership the United States might give to the world?

CHAPTER 20

Prayer Groups in the Community

Do NOT ALLOW A PRAYER GROUP TO BECOME AN ESCAPE FROM taking sacrificial, responsible action. A prayer group is not an ivory tower into which we can retreat from the necessity of grasping the nettle. United prayer never fails to lead to some kind of constructive action. It seems to sharpen and focus all of our faculties, and we are led to do things which ordinarily we would never think of doing.

In November, 1952, a member of our parish, an instrument man in the Homestead Plant of the United States Steel Company, had the idea that small groups of men meeting together for prayer in various parts of the plant would make for better human relations as well as for better working relations in the plant. He figured that this would not only help his fellow workers in their personal lives but reduce friction and increase output for the company.

His idea caught on. By December of 1952 a large group was meeting; by June, 1953, another was added. In September the Pittsburgh *Press* felt it of enough significance to publish a story, and in October, 1953, *Fortune* magazine included it in a feature called "Business Men On Their Knees."

If you have ever visited a great steel plant you may appreciate the daring and drama involved in any attempt to meet for prayer in one of the half-mile-long open hearth sheds lined with great furnaces filled with white-hot molten metal. There is the constant noise of furnaces being filled or others being tapped and pouring out great streams of burning liquid into huge ladles. These, in turn, are tipped into twelve-foot molds, which overflow with golden flame and showers of sparks.

There is the clash and clang of the rolling mills, where the enormous red hot hunks of steel are rolled out and cut up into the desired width and thickness, amidst sizzling jets of steam.

There are the tool and instrument shops and the huge loading sheds, where giant hooks are continually lifting, piling, and sorting enormous flat finished squares and oblongs of cold, blue steel, and loading them onto freight cars for shipment.

The following is Dave's account of how these men, in these unlikely places, have proceeded with their prayer meetings and what has happened:

The original Homestead group, which was started in November, 1952, has continued to meet every Thursday morning in the Pyrometer Room of the Power and Fuel Department, using sometimes a tape-recorded talk or sermonette written by ministers of various faiths or by laymen, or often a talk by one of the group.

Stanley, a Roman Catholic, father of five children, and a

top-rated instrument man, decided to build himself a telescope, which he took with him when he visited friends, and while they looked at the heavens through his handiwork he told them what he had learned about the stars and the glory of God. He did a lot of good with his telescope, and one day came to me and said he would like to make a recording, telling the group how he felt about God.

For Stan this took a lot of gumption, because he was quite shy. However, he made a fine recording and the story was retold later in many other parts of the mill by instrument men who had heard it that morning. Stan has become one of the pillars of the program.

Matt, the water inspector for the Homestead Works, is a leader in the Pyrometer Room. In addition to his everyday tasks at the mill, Matt has devoted a great deal of time to the prayer program and the spiritual needs of the men in the mill. His talks and prayers on Thursday mornings have been inspired, especially one which was recorded recently. As the men went about the mill repairing instruments they told others about the wonderful story they had heard that morning. As the news spread, there came requests for a copy of Matt's talk. They came from the open hearth, the rolling mills, the maintenance shops, the various offices and even from men working on the railroad which serves the plant. A plant policeman stopped me as I left the plant three weeks later and asked me if I could possibly get him a copy of the talk.

Matt has given out about four hundred mimeographed copies and is still getting requests for more. As a result of the programs and Matt's part in them, envelopes containing requests for prayer have been left on his desk, and they still appear.

A very good-looking young man who had lost what little faith he did have in three years at a too strict church college has found a new concept of God and life as a result of the program. Tony worked with me for four months and we found time to talk together about God, and at the last to pray together about our individual and collective problems.

One Wednesday morning, after working all night in the

open hearth, Tony climbed into my car and went with me to Latrobe to visit the plant of the Stupakoff Ceramic and Manufacturing Company and hear their morning prayer program, "Meditation Moments at Stupakoff." He got some sleep as we drove home but it wasn't until 2 P.M. that I delivered a very tired but happy young assistant fuel engineer to his wife. Tony is now a vestryman in his church, and his reborn faith guides his family life, his mill activities, and I believe plays a great part in vestry meetings.

Tony told me one morning about 1:30 A.M. that he felt he should talk to the men some Thursday morning. I suggested several topics, but he said he had his own and I had better wait and see what came of it. He held the men enthralled with the story of what God had come to mean to him and his family.

Henry, a machinist, started to pray about what he might do to bring God and faith to Homestead. Three days later, after talking to many of his fellow workmen, he initiated a prayer group in one corner of the balcony of Number One Machine Shop. Sixteen men gathered at 7:45 A.M., fifteen minutes before starting time, to hear Henry, a solidly built, gray-haired German who came to this country after World War I, read from the Bible and pray. Henry's group has continued to meet every Wednesday morning from 7:45 until 8:00 A.M.

Another young man, Chuck, has taken hold of the idea of brotherly love and putting Christianity to work in our everyday life by actually going out in the mill and talking and showing men what God has come to mean to him. He has reorganized a defunct Men's Club at his church and has had six meetings. The membership covers the entire range of ages, and in their meetings they are studying the fundamental aspects of the church.

Several men from the group have appeared in Calvary and other churches on Sunday mornings, after having told me that before we began our morning meetings it had been years since they were last in church.

A number of very bad domestic situations have been happily resolved. Confusion and indecision in the minds of many men have been cleared up, and the knowledge has been firmly implanted in the general consciousness of people all over the plant that God hears our prayers, that prayer is the key to all situations, and that we can love and understand our fellow men.

In a small Maryland town a group of young married women met regularly for prayer until the war in Korea dispersed them. One evening early in June, 1950, just after the outbreak of the Korean War, they were sitting in a circle in a quiet walled garden of an old, ivy-covered church. They began telling one another of the ways in which their time of united prayer the week before had helped them and enabled them to help others during that week.

One of their number, who had lived through two personal tragedies, burst out with: "Last week I didn't see how I could stand another thing after all I've been through, and, on top of it all, this war and Bill [her only son] of draft age. This group has come to my rescue. Without the steadying encouragement of your prayers and fellowship I don't see how I could go on."

Two others told of the conversations they had had with young married women at market and at the swimming pool during the week. A great army center for the development of bacteriological warfare lies on the edge of their town. Many of their young friends, wives of the scientific and Army research men stationed there, came to these young women, frantic with fear and resentment.

"Perhaps because of our prayers here we can become stabilizers to our friends!" said one of the prayer group. "I've never had so many people come to me and pour out their troubles as have come this week."

"Yes," another said, "and because of what I've learned in this group I find I can help my friends regain their perspective and calm down."

Not long ago a most remarkable document arrived in the mail of a United States senator. It was entitled, "A Résumé of Our Year of Evangelistic Work of the Chinese Christian Women's Prayer Group," which came from Taipeh Taiwan, Formosa. It described the five-member women's prayer group formed by Mme. Chiang Kai-shek soon after her return to Formosa in January, 1950. Their purpose was to stimulate all Christian women in Formosa to pray earnestly and devotedly for a spiritual revival among the women of Formosa and China, so that they might become spiritually equipped to reform society and build new homes in a new China.

Every Wednesday these women met for prayer, opened by a period of Bible study. Out of this group emerged five family prayer groups, three family Bible classes, and four Sunday schools numbering four hundred and fifty children, as well as twenty centers of Christian work. From it also came a committee to organize an evangelistic program and establish chaplains in six army hospitals, where three thousand wounded have been reached and twenty thousand soldiers have heard the Gospel. The members of the prayer group have visited the hospitals, and at Christmas saw to it that there were Christmas trees and gifts for the men in every ward.

Over eleven hundred people were baptized as a result of this spirited action, and two touching stories are told of the help brought to wounded men. One man who had lost the power of speech was converted, and spoke immediately. Four young officers who were badly wounded and suffering great pain had agreed to commit suicide, but after hearing the chaplain preach, they turned their bottle of poison over to him and were baptized instead.

Group prayer sets up a positive chain reaction of which no one can foresee the end. Whether we meet as a family or in prayer study groups, or meet in prayer, though not in person, "for special intentions," where two of us agree to pray secretly for some particular concern, or meet at the altar rail, the result is always the same—power is released, people are healed and changed, hope is reborn, and, above all, we do our small share in fulfilling Jesus' vision: "That they all may be one; as thou, Father, art in me, and I in thee, that they also may be one in us; that the world may believe that thou has sent me" (John 17:21).

The Anglican Bishop of Croyden, England, describes a beautiful Easter ceremony which took place in Athens recently:

> One Easter Eve I stood in a crowded square in Athens. A vast concourse of people waited there, silent, expectant. On a dais in the middle of the square stood the King of Greece, the Prime Minister, the Cabinet, and all the leaders of the people. Above us the stars looked down from a cloudless sky; the cathedral loomed dark and mysterious against the moonlight.
>
> And then its great doors were flung open. The bells rang out the chimes of midnight. The Archbishop of Athens walked slowly down the steps. In his hand gleamed the light of a candle. In the silence he mounted the rostrum and lit the candle of the King of Greece. So the light was passed on—from King to Prime Minister, from Prime Minister to Cabinet; and soon the whole square was ablaze with countless points of light.
>
> "Christ is risen," cried the Archbishop.
>
> "He is risen indeed," shouted the crowd in reply. And as the shout died away they ran through the streets to carry the light of faith and hope into the dark world of paganism and sin.[20]

Those of us who pray and unite in prayer become not only lighters of lights, but carriers of the light. In the words of Father Keller of "The Christophers," "As soon as more people are lighting lights than turning them off, the darkness will disappear."[21]

CHAPTER 21

The Power of United Worship

ARCHBISHOP TEMPLE SAYS THIS: "THE WORLD WILL BE SAVED BY only one thing, and that is worship."[22] Dr. Nels Ferré says, "A praying church is a worshiping church, a worshiping church is a working church."

The World Day of Prayer is held on the first Friday of Lent by women in ninety nations throughout the world, and is in a sense symbolic of the power of the praying and worshiping church. Imagine on this day, from sunrise to sunset, women around the world gathering in kraals, grass huts, forest glades, chapels, and cathedrals to offer their prayers of praise and petition to their living Lord!

In 1949, for the first time a World Day of Prayer service was held in the great Marienkirche in the Soviet sector of Berlin. An eyewitness sent the following moving account:

Today I have had an experience which I shall probably never have again in my lifetime, and I must tell you about it. . . . First you must come to Berlin, to the doors of the Marienkirche. . . .

This is the *Weltgebetstag der Frauen,* the World Day of Prayer for Women. Four years ago such a world prayer day was unknown in Germany, and then Mrs. Arthur Siebans, the wife of the pastor of the American Church in Berlin, arrived. She felt that this movement, world-wide, should find a place also in this great city. From very humble beginnings, together with only a few German women, she organized the first *Weltgebetstag der Frauen.*

As we drove here from our home in the American sector, we saw a sign—"You are now entering the British sector of Berlin," and then another—"You are now leaving the British sector of Berlin." That meant we were entering the Russian sector of Berlin. . . . Because we shall park outside the church, we feel rather safe in taking our car today. We would not park outside a private dwelling, it might be too dangerous for the people within.

The Marienkirche is perhaps the largest church in Berlin. It has a very long nave and a deep chancel. Partly destroyed during the war, it has been somewhat restored and whitewashed within. It is very beautiful.

And yet we cannot go through the doors before you know something more, for coming right out of America you have not yet felt the fear which is here in the east sector and in the east zone. First you should hear the words of a fine young Christian who said to me: "Fear crowds in upon us; it fills our days and our nights, and when you are hungry and cold, and dare not speak, it is hard to keep hope alive in the heart."

And then you should also know something about the women who lead today's prayer service. It is too dangerous to name them. All of them have suffered. Most of them have husbands who resisted during the Nazi times. All of them today are giving their lives to help their brethren. . . .

Now you and I enter the little anteroom off from the church hall, where we who take part in this service bow our heads and pray for God's blessings. Then the wonderful organ music begins and we quietly walk up to the front of the church through the long aisles, past the packed pews, trying to overcome the emotions which crowd upon us as we see this great old church, newly restored, whitewashed, full to overflowing with three thousand women!

Are you standing beside me? Can you see them, these women, drably dressed, white-faced with tired eyes, many standing because there are not enough places to sit in this cold, unheated church, and each of them here to pray! We know that all the world over, today, "from the rising of the sun to the going down thereof," women are gathering in churches to pray for peace. . . .

First we pray for forgiveness for the sins of not caring about our brother, for waiting for peace to come from somewhere else and not seeking it by having Christ in our hearts. Then we pray for our churches, our brethren, the poor, the sick, the fearful. Then we pray for our world in its great distress, and through all the prayers we pray for Christ to be our personal friend and Saviour, realizing that He gives peace. . . .

Two women choirs sing beautifully, and then it is time for the meditation and prayers. Now we rise to sing *Ein Feste Burg ist Unser Gott* (A Mighty Fortress Is Our God), and we know in faith that these prayers can be answered. . . .

Outside the rain is falling, and the women in their thin old shoes start home to cheerless rooms, black, clammy bread, and no heat. We have brought a friend with us, a woman who has suffered unbelievably during the war years. She sits in the car beside us as we drive her to the Alexanderplatz station and weeps. "Thank you for letting me come with you. It was to be in heaven! To think there are still that many people who pray, that there are still good men in the world. Truly, this is for me a Holy Day. God bless you!!"

Could this possibly be one of the secrets of the spiritual strength and courage of the people of East Berlin—for this great service of worship is but the outward and visible sign of the secret spirit of worship kept alive in thousands of individual hearts throughout the whole world, and especially in those nations in which the Kremlin has sought to extinguish it.

We all need to become part of the corporate worship of the Church of the world. We sing, "Like a Mighty Army Moves the Church of God," but how many of us join that army so that it may become truly mighty?

If Archbishop Temple is right, and I believe he is, the supreme purpose of the Church is to foster this spirit of worship so that the world may be saved. This cannot happen, however, so long as we refuse to take any part in the total life of the Church, the heart of which is worship.

Some of us may balk at this proposal. There are ninety-two million enrolled church members in this country, which leaves about sixty-eight million unaffiliated with the Christian Church. People, when approached, give many reasons for not enrolling in the church.

A friend of mine, the Rev. Grant H. Elford, while on a trip to the Near East with a fellow Methodist minister, the Rev. Ronald Merideth, tells the following story:

Dr. Merideth and I were talking about the various reasons why people don't attend church, and how weak most of them are. Dr. Merideth started off on a frivolous tack by saying that "some folks say they don't come to church because the pastor never calls on them. . . . Well, the manager of a theater doesn't call on them either, but those folks don't stay away from the movies!" I countered with: "Yes, and every time I go to the theater they ask me for money, too." . . . Then followed repartee wherein some other ideas came out.

That night I jotted these "gems" about movie going down in my notebook, and when I got home I set them down, and added a few more, which I published in my church bulletin.

The local newspaper editor picked them up, and in a week or so a large city paper printed them on the editorial page. A few weeks later, *Newsweek* magazine called and asked if they could have a story and print "My Ten Reasons." Soon the article was read on a nation-wide radio program, and later it appeared in *Reader's Digest*. The reasons are as follows:

1. The shows are held in the evenings, and that's the only time I am able to be at home with the family.

2. I don't think they have very good music at the theater.

3. I don't always agree with what I hear and see.

4. I don't care for some of the people I see and meet at the theater.

5. The performance lasts too long; I can't sit still for an hour and three quarters.

6. I went so much as a child, I've decided I've had all the entertainment I need.

7. Not all folks live up to the high moral standards of the films.

8. Every time I go they ask me for money.

9. I did go a few times, but no one spoke to me. Those who go there aren't very friendy.

10. The manager of the theater never called on me.[23]

These satirical excuses give a pretty accurate description of those we make for not going to church. In the face of a world situation which threatens our faith as well as our freedom, these excuses are, to say the least, immature.

The Communists have their church; the Communist party is an international organization seeking to control the world. "Hell knows no fury like the prophets of a secular religion become the priest kings of a Utopian state." The priest kings of Communism were Lenin and Stalin; the religion of Communism is dialectic materialism. All sincere Communists join their church and pledge themselves to do everything in their power to spread their dark faith. They do not have the freedom to make excuses.

Loyalty to country, essential as it is, is not enough to offset this dynamic religion that is sweeping the world. A passionate dedication to freedom is not enough—freedom is only a by-product of faith. Even faith alone is not enough, and must have a vehicle through which to express itself and a leader to whom to pledge itself.

That leader is Christ, and that vehicle is the Christian Church. The Christian Church holds its charter from Christ Himself. Its declaration of faith is the Creed. Its universal prayer, spoken in every language on earth, is the Lord's Prayer. It is the one great international institution, standing like an immense road block in the path of Communism. It is the one organization that Communism fears and has pledged itself to destroy. The Communist leaders know well that passionate belief in God and the ideal of establishing His Kingdom on earth is the only world force strong enough to conquer them. Therefore, when the Communists take over a nation they soon find a good excuse for liquidating the leaders of the church and closing these houses of worship.

Our Christian faith is the dynamic of our democracy. The precious freedoms which we Americans so much enjoy are the flowers springing from the root of our Christian faith. Neglect the root, and the flowers soon will wither and die. If you refuse to water the root of faith by failing to go to church and joining with others in worship you are in real danger of being one of those giving lip service to democracy while refusing to make it live.

Imagine the towns and cities of this great nation with no church spires piercing our blue skies, no place to go to have our babies baptized, our marriages blessed, our dead buried. This could happen here. It is happening with frightening speed in other lands. The Church could be destroyed by Communism. It is lukewarm, indifferent, undisciplined Christians who will sell it out, if ever it is sold out.

I am persuaded that if the majority of our millions of non-churchgoers knew what the Church has contributed to our civilization, what it stands for in the present and offers us in the future, they would enroll in its ranks.

What has the Christian Church contributed to civilization? First, it has been loyal to its founder, the Lord Jesus Christ. Through a turbulent two thousand years of history there have always been those in the church who truly worshiped and enshrined Him in their hearts. As a result, faith in Him and His real meaning for mankind has been kept bright and shining. The Church has nurtured and cultivated the worship of Him, His Father, and His Holy Spirit. In the services of the Church Year the great events of His life and death, the resurrection, ascension, and Pentecost have been dramatized. In the season of Advent we prepare to receive Him. At Christmas we re-enact, in carols and pageantry and story, the tender account of His nativity. In Epiphany we re-enact His early years. In Lent we observe the forty days of His fasting, temptation, and prayer, followed by the climactic drama of Holy Week, when we follow Him into Jerusalem, to the Garden of Gethsemane, and up to Calvary, until we stand before the empty tomb on Easter morning. Then come the Ascension season and Pentecost, the commemoration of the birthday of the Church, when His Living Holy Spirit came into His followers and His Church was born. The long Trinity season reminds us continually of the threefold function of God. He is our Father, our Redeemer, and our Empowerer. The sweep of this mighty drama of redemption is re-enacted for us every single year in the weekly worship services of the Church, and has been for two thousand unbroken years.

As we come to Morning Worship shall we remember, with gratitude, that the Church has not allowed one iota of this glory to be forgotten or fade from man's memory?

Second, the Church has kept alive the spirit of worship in the world. But what is worship?

Worship is a candle in the act of being lighted.

Worship is the soul standing silent before the mysteries.

Worship is an eager heart seeking for the love that never fails.

Worship is man climbing the altar stairs to God.

The world would be poor indeed without the great oratories and anthems by Bach, Gounod, Handel, Mozart, Beethoven, Tchaikovsky, and a host of others, whose gift of music has found its most inspired expression in those paeans of love and praise to their Lord and King.

Our Protestant hymns, which express all our spiritual moods, were written by men whose experience of life and suffering and death have been transformed through worship into songs of triumph.

Such songs and hymns as "Dear Lord and Father of Mankind," "God of our Fathers," "For All the Saints," and "A Mighty Fortress Is Our God" are the heritage of the free nations. They are a part of the life blood of worship.

Imagine a world without the great cathedrals of Europe —expressions in exquisitely carved stone and jewel-like glass of the spirit of worship of the men and women of the Middle Ages.

Imagine our civilization denied the glorious religious art and poetry of medieval times and the Renaissance. All of this magnificent, creative expression was the way in which the artists and poets of that day worshiped. The "Sistine Madonna," the Sistine Chapel, the frescoes of Giotto, the paintings of Fra Angelico, the "Last Supper" of Leonardo da Vinci, the matchless madonnas of Flanders, the poetry of Dante would never have been bequeathed to us if the gifts of these great geniuses had not been their expression of worship.

Our modern system of education was born in the hearts of worshiping sons of the Church. In the Middle Ages the light of learning was jealously guarded in the monasteries, and flowered in the great medieval universities of Bologne, Paris, and Padua. Every one of the great private colleges and schools in our own country was founded by some worshiping son of the Church. Christian education went hand in hand with evangelism in the establishment of our American Christian culture. Most of our universities were founded and established by churchmen.

Wherever the light of learning and literacy has gone in the world you will find that worshiping Christians have started it. The Christian colleges of Asia and the Near East are among the most powerful bulwarks against Communism in those lands.

The Church likewise has pioneered the social services. Hospitals for the care of the sick have been brought into being by churchmen, and in the Eastern countries were manned and supported by people who worshiped God through this sacrificial means.

It was a Quakeress, Elizabeth Fry, who with intrepid courage broke through the prejudices and ignorance of early nineteenth-century England regarding prisons and prison life, and became the mother of modern prison reform.

It was a Swiss Protestant and devoted churchman who felt called of God to plant the seeds of the Red Cross—the only international institution dedicated to the alleviation of human distress.

All of our great networks of social services, all our government agencies to care for the aged, the poor, and the sick, gained their original impetus from little bands of church people who said their prayers and then sought in their own communities to follow the example of Christ in helping those no one else would help.

Modern psychology had its birth in the Church. One of Jesus' greatest acts was the casting out of devils, in other words, the healing of the mentally ill. The early services of the Church contained special services of worship for the mentally ill.

Such is the worship of the Church and the result of that worship. We should be so proud of our Christian heritage, so grateful to our spiritual forebears, out of whose blood, toil, sweat, and tears have come this great gift known as Christian civilization, that we should seek to carry on this great heritage from sheer gratitude! For we are the inheritors of the spiritual experience, the spiritual power, the spiritual heroism, the spiritual creativity and worship of four thousand years of history.

We Americans have a strong sense of family. Many people in this country are justly proud of their ancestors, their family traditions, their family customs, their family's contribution to the building of this country.

The Church is our Christian family. It preserves the records of our Christian family tree. Our manners, our customs, even our common, everyday expressions have been bequeathed to us by our spiritual forebears in the Church. The genius of the Christian family, the romance of the Christian family, the great deeds of the Christian family, are all preserved and carried on for us by the Church. When we go to church to worship together we realize with a deep sense of joy and security that we are part of a great, living company who through the centuries have come together as we are coming together, to worship a living God, not a dead ideal.

What do you do when you go to church? Do you really participate in its service, or are you merely a spectator Christian? Why not try an experiment? Next Sunday try to participate in every part of the service. Sing the hymns with your whole heart, give your full attention to the Psalms as you read them. Pray silently with the minister as he prays, and, above all, pray for him as he preaches. In other words, enter in and worship! Bring your prayer list with you—the sick, the troubled; bring your worries and fears, and as you worship with all those others you will feel the peace of God stealing in and the power of God giving you new vigor and confidence. You will hear the word of God with new ears, and read the words of God with new understanding. If you really participated in this Sunday worship you would begin to understand all that it means; you might even find that it sets a new pace not only for your week but for your life.

If you are experiencing sorrow or sickness, fear or insecurity, if you do not know where to turn or where to go, come to the church. Go in, kneel down in the quietness of it as millions have done before you. God will meet you there, and take your hand and lift you up as He has done for desperate and heartsick men and women down through the centuries. He will put you in touch with His people, who will give you the comfort and love and fellowship and sense of belonging that you need.

There is a beautiful stained-glass window in the chancel of a church in a great city. Each exquisite medallion of this window tells the story of Jesus' birth, and underneath, in letters of crimson and blue, on a shield of gold, are etched the words: "I am come that they might have life, and that they might have it more abundantly" (John 10:10).

Into this chancel, lighted by the glorious windows, a young man and woman came, hand in hand, to kneel before the altar and take part in the Lord's Supper. It was Christmas Eve. The church was filled with the haunting, remembered refrains of the age-old Christmas carols celebrating the birth of Christ.

These two had come, not long before, out of the masses of gay, attractive, irresponsible young pagans to seek a living faith. Like millions of others, they were appalled and frightened by the insecurity of our chaotic world. Their lives, filled with friends, pleasure, material success, were strangely empty. They knew instinctively that something was missing.

Quite by chance they met a Christian minister who had something. In fact, he not only had something, he knew Someone. Someone whom he assured them held all the answers to the questions that were bothering them. The young couple did not quite understand what he meant, but they trusted him. The day they met him the minister had asked them to come to church on Christmas Eve, and here they were.

In the beauty and tenderness of the glorious service of worship they suddenly felt the realness of the Person whose birthday was being celebrated. They felt, too, the nearly overwhelming reality of the millions of average people like themselves, who through the ages had thronged to the great cathedrals, the tiny village churches, to celebrate His birthday and join the shepherds and the wise men in honoring Him. Among these millions there must have been many like themselves who were in need of help and guidance.

After the service, they sought out the minister and timidly asked him if he would kneel at the altar with them for a few moments. The three of them came forward, and in the dark, warm chancel, beautiful with the candlelight throwing into relief a statue of Christ with His arms outstretched, the young couple simply and haltingly pledged to Him their loyalty, and asked Him if He would allow them to become part of His family.

That evening they knew for the first time the meaning of the words inscribed underneath the Nativity window. Suddenly they felt free, with a glorious, tingling freedom, as crisp and sparkling as the brilliant December night. They felt, too, that they had found a family, that they had found a Person whom they could worship, and a cause to which they could whole-heartedly give their loyalty, and entrust their lives.

Nailed to the main doorway of a lovely colonial church, set on a hilltop in the rolling farm country of Maryland, is an invitation that is half a prayer:

Friend, you have come to this church.
No man entering a house ignores Him who dwells in it.
This is the House of God. He is here.
Pray, then, to Him who loves you and awaits your greeting.
Give thanks for those who in past ages built this place to His glory,
And for those who dying that we might live have preserved for
    us our heritage.
Ask that we who now live may build the spiritual fabric of the
    nation in truth, beauty and goodness.
And as we draw near the Father through our Lord Jesus Christ,
May we draw near to one another in brotherhood.

Conclusion

THIS LITTLE BOOK IS A TRUMPET CALL TO FAITH AND ACTION. IN IT we have taken a fearless look at the terrifying world forces which are threatening our freedom, our happiness, our lives.

I do not believe that Communism and total mutual destruction are the wave of the future.

The real conqueror of Communism and its threat of destruction by hydrogen bomb could prove to be the triumphant faith and action of the people of prayer.

We hope that this book will inspire you to join us, the great growing army of God's people who believe that nothing is too hard for Him, and that with Him as our leader we will prove that spiritual force is still the first force in the world, and that Our Lord's vision, "Thy Kingdom Come," is not an empty dream, but a glorious possibility.

Dr. Fritz Kunkel, the well-known psychotherapist, says, "Watching the religious development of our time, no one can say that this is the agony of a dying faith. It looks more like a beginning. Christianity, it seems, is coming of age. It might prove to be the decisive factor in the future of man-kind——. That Christianity will finally conquer the earth is certain, and every real Christian will participate in this success even though he may actually perish in a concentration camp."

We the people of prayer may feel very small and ineffective as we face the potential destructive power of evil, and yet Jesus' promise is to us, as it was to His handful of trembling disciples on the hills of Galilee, "Fear not little flock, it is your Father's good pleasure to give you the kingdom."

Acknowledgments

1. Dr. Elton Trueblood, *The Life We Prize*, Harper & Brothers, New York.
2. *Ibid.*
3. Dr. E. Stanley Jones, *The Way to Power and Poise*, Abingdon Press, New York and Nashville, Tennessee.
4. Used by permission of Dr. Theodore Ferris, Rector Trinity Church, Boston.
5. Father George, *God's Underground*, Appleton-Century Crofts, New York City.
6. Dr. William Temple, *Readings in St. John's Gospel*, St. Martin's Press, New York City.
7. Dr. E. Stanley Jones, *The Way to Power and Poise*, Abingdon Press, New York, and Nashville, Tennessee.
8. Dr. William Temple, *Readings in St. John's Gospel*, St. Martin's Press, New York City.
9. *Ibid.*
10. Used by permission of Agnes Sanford.
11. Harry F. Gerecke, "I Walked to the Gallows with the Nazi Chiefs," *Saturday Evening Post* (Sept. 1, 1951), p. 17.
12. Dr. William Temple, *Readings in St. John's Gospel*, St. Martin's Press, New York City.
13. Dr. Norman Vincent Peale, *The Power of Positive Thinking*, Prentice-Hall, New York City.
14. *Ibid.*
15. "Faith That Works," *The Calvary Evangel*, New York City.

16. *Ibid.* Used by permission of *The Calvary Evangel,* New York City.

17. Used by permission of Bishop Richard S. M. Emrich.

18. Andrew Murray, *With Christ in the School of Prayer,* Fleming H. Revell, Westwood, N. J.

19. *Ibid.*

20. "Faith That Works," *The Calvary Evangel,* New York City.

21. Used by permission of Father Keller of "The Christophers."

22. Dr. William Temple, *Readings in St. John's Gospel,* St. Martin's Press, New York City.

23. "The Ten Reasons," used by permission of Dr. Grant Elford.